Negotiating
FOR
DUMMIES®
PORTABLE EDITION

by Michael C. Donaldson

WILEY

John Wiley & Sons, Inc.

Negotiating For Dummies, Portable Edition

Published by
John Wiley & Sons, Inc.
111 River St.
Hoboken, NJ 07030-5774
www.wiley.com

Copyright © 2012 by John Wiley & Sons, Inc., Hoboken, New Jersey

Published by John Wiley & Sons, Inc., Hoboken, New Jersey

For general information on our other products and services, please contact our Customer Care Department within the U.S. at 877-762-2974, outside the U.S. at 317-572-3993, or fax 317-572-4002.

For technical support, please visit www.wiley.com/techsupport.

Wiley also publishes its books in a variety of electronic formats and by print-on-demand. Some content that appears in standard print versions of this book may not be available in other formats. For more information about Wiley products, visit us at www.wiley.com.

ISBN 978-1-118-30715-1 (pbk); ISBN 978-1-118-30717-5 (ebk); ISBN 978-1-118-30719-9 (ebk); ISBN 978-1-118-30718-2 (ebk)

Manufactured in the United States of America

10 9 8 7 6 5 4 3 2

Publisher's Acknowledgments

Project Editor: Kathleen Dobie

Composition Services: Indianapolis Composition Services Department

Cover Photos: © iStockphoto.com / Mark Wragg

WILEY

Contents

Introduction

. . . .

You negotiate all day long, in every situation you encounter — with your boss or your employees, with your vendors or your clients, with your spouse or your kids, with the plumber who comes to your house to fix your leaky faucet. All of these relationships call for constant negotiation.

A *negotiation* is any communication in which you are attempting to achieve the approval, acquiescence, or action of someone else. The lessons in this book apply to both the once-in-a-lifetime, million-dollar deals and the everyday, one-minute life negotiations.

Who Needs to Read This Book?

Everyone.

Face it, you negotiate all day long, and you can do a much better job of it. No matter how you perceive your skills today, they can be stronger tomorrow. And your progress can start with this book.

The mission of this book is to help you to negotiate from strength. Understanding the six essential skills used in every negotiation transforms you into a confident and successful negotiator. After you master the six basic skills of negotiating and achieve a position of strength, every tough situation you encounter becomes easier to analyze and conquer.

Foolish Assumptions

This book is for you whether you are

- ✔ Beginning a career, or just looking to brush up your skills
- ✔ A pushover who never seems to get your way, or a master negotiator — widely admired but constantly striving to improve

✔ Unemployed and want a job, or employed and want a raise

✔ A teacher searching for a way to get your students to do what you want them to do, or a parent wanting to talk more convincingly with your children

✔ A team player who wants to have more input during negotiating sessions, or a team leader going for a specific win in your next negotiation

About This Book

This book is not about tricks or one-upmanship. This book gives you guidance by breaking negotiations down into their basic elements.

Think of this book as your friend and coach, someone to go to when you have a question about negotiating. This book identifies each basic skill and then demonstrates its use in every situation. If you practice these skills enough, you can become a world-class negotiator, turning the basic strokes of a negotiation into winning power strokes.

How This Book Is Organized

This book covers the basic negotiating skills in ten chapters:

✔ **Chapter 1, Negotiating for Life:** This chapter goes through the six essential skills for successful negotiating. The first of these is preparation and Chapter 1 shows you how to prepare yourself for a negotiation, figure out the other side, and put the negotiation in context. All this preparation sounds like a lot of work, but it's the key to real power in any negotiation.

✔ **Chapter 2, Setting and Enforcing Limits:** You need to set your goals and define your limits *before* the actual negotiation begins. They carry you right to the end of the negotiation, enabling you to decide when to close a deal and when to walk away.

✔ **Chapter 3, Asking the Right Questions:** Asking questions leads you to knowledge and putting that knowledge to use can lead to a successful outcome. This chapter covers the when, what, and how of asking questions during a negotiation.

✔ **Chapter 4, Listening with All Your Senses:** Listening may be the most underrated skill, but being able to hear and understand what your counterpart says is essential if you want to negotiate successfully. Body language can be just as expressive as the spoken word and this chapter covers listening with all your senses.

✔ **Chapter 5, Being Crystal Clear: Telling It Like It Is:** Everybody talks so much each day that clarity sometimes gets lost. Turn to this chapter if you want to make each word count and make sure that people hear you every time you speak.

✔ **Chapter 6, Pushing the Pause Button to Turn Off the Hot Buttons:** Turn here to find out how emotions can influence and upset a negotiation; then discover how to curtail your emotions using your pause button. Like the pause button on your DVD player, this essential skill enables you to freeze-frame the negotiation and take a break — a great way to keep your emotional distance.

✔ **Chapter 7, Closing the Deal and Feeling Good About It:** Closure is a separate skill that you must develop if you are to become successful in every negotiation you undertake. This chapter tells you how.

✔ **Chapter 8, When the Deal Just Won't Seem to Close:** Of course, all kinds of mishaps can keep a deal from closing. This chapter discusses those situations in which you feel you have done everything right, and yet the deal still won't close — and it offers suggestions for solutions.

✔ **Chapter 9, Blind Negotiating via Telephone and E-mail:** The telephone and Internet have changed the way we communicate. This chapter contains a lot of helpful hints and tips to follow when negotiating electronically.

✔ **Chapter 10, Ten Personality Traits of Top Negotiators:** You, too, can develop the qualities top negotiators share.

Icons Used in This Book

Check out the margins of this book and you find lots of little pictures. These icons guide you to the information you crave.

This icon marks the dirty tricks sharks try to play on you. Don't fall prey to these pitfalls — and avoid using these nasty tactics yourself.

Just looking for the bottom line? This icon emphasizes information that you should absolutely, positively keep in mind at all times if you want to be a successful negotiator.

This icon denotes honest tricks of the trade, shortcuts, and loopholes. I've stumbled across plenty of tips that you may want to have at your fingertips. Look for these icons to save time, money, and face in your next negotiation.

Where to Go from Here

Look through Chapter 1 to get an overview of the six essential skills you need in every negotiation. Then turn to the chapter that covers that particular skill in depth.

Most people won't start in the area in which they need the most help. They usually choose their favorite area — the area about which they are confident. That's okay. Even your strongest area can get stronger. Then, as you shift your focus to your weaker areas, you enjoy the greatest amount of progress.

The most important point to consider right now is that you're already headed toward the winner's circle. The most successful people in life are those who continue to grow. The fact that you have this book in your hand now puts you into that realm. It's not how much you know that counts, but how much you are willing to add after you "know it all."

Chapter 1

Negotiating for Life

In This Chapter

▶ Applying the six basic skills of negotiating

▶ Handling unique negotiations

*N*egotiating is not a skill to take out once in a while when you have to make a deal. Negotiating is a way to get what you want out of life. You negotiate all day long, whether it's with your co-workers, your spouse, or your kids.

Any time you ask someone to say yes or to do something for you or to get out of the way so you can do it, you are negotiating. If you're attempting to resolve a dispute, agree on a course of action, or bargain for individual advantage, you are in a negotiation, like it or not. The goal is to reach a resolution that is acceptable to you and that will work for both parties. If that's not possible, try to find such an agreement elsewhere.

If you think of negotiating as a sport, you can use this book as a manual to improve your game. For example, if you are a good listener, but need help in setting limits, read Chapter 2. For tips on how to close the deal, go to Chapter 7 — or Chapter 8 if you just can't get to the close. Of course, you can always read the book from cover to cover. But most people read this chapter for an overview and then skip around the book.

As your skills grow, you will take charge of *all* the negotiations you face in your life. Even if your dreams or your paycheck seem to hinge on forces beyond your control, you can create a master plan for your life and achieve your dreams — one negotiation at a time.

The Six Basic Skills of Negotiating

No matter how large or small, how important or minor, how near or far, a negotiation involves six basic skills. After you understand how you can use these skills in a negotiation, you will use them every time you sit down at the negotiating table.

The skills you need to be a successful negotiator in your everyday life are the same skills powerful businesspeople use during major international and industrial negotiations. Sure, you can refine these skills with additional techniques and strategies, and you enhance them with your own style and personality. But only these six skills are essential:

- ✔ Thorough preparation
- ✔ The ability to set limits and goals
- ✔ Good listening skills
- ✔ Clarity of communication
- ✔ Knowing how and when to push your pause button
- ✔ Knowing how to close a deal

The six basic negotiating skills apply to all areas of life. They can empower you to be happier and more successful in your life by helping you gain more respect, reach better agreements with your business partners and family, and maintain more control in your negotiations.

Prepare

Preparation is the bedrock of negotiation success. You cannot be overprepared for a negotiation. Whether you are involved in a business or personal negotiation, you must be thoroughly prepared to achieve your goals. Heck, you have to be well prepared just to know what your goals are.

In any negotiation, you must prepare in three areas:

   ✔ Yourself

   ✔ The other person

   ✔ The market

Pay special attention to the first point because you are the most important person in the room. The second item will change as your negotiations change. The third point deserves your lifelong attention.

Prepare yourself

Preparing yourself for a negotiation means knowing yourself and what you want out of life. This step takes some reflection and some planning. With adequate preparation, you boost your confidence and your performance during a negotiation. Know your strengths and weaknesses.

What is your life plan? In a perfect world, what will you be doing in three years? This long-range thinking about your own life provides a context for every negotiation you have. After you create a vision of your future, create a plan that includes specific steps to turn your vision into reality. Your negotiations are likely to go astray if you don't prepare your personal, long-range game plan *before* entering the negotiating room.

You also have to prepare yourself for specific negotiating situations. The better you know your own needs, the more easily you can do this. For example, if you're not a morning person, don't let someone schedule a conference call for 7:30 in the morning.

Prepare for the other person

When you find out who you'll be sitting across from at the negotiating table, research that person. Knowing about the other person can help you build rapport, and you can walk into a room with the comfort and knowledge of having some background on your opponent. One of the most common instances where you should do some research on other person is before a job interview. Perhaps you and your interviewer share a similar past experience. When you show that you know a fact or two about the other person from having done your research, you usually score points with the interviewer. In a negotiation, showing that you've prepared for the other person also serves as an ice-breaker before getting down to the nitty-gritty.

Besides these obvious social benefits, knowledge about the other person lets you know what you're up against. Is this person reasonable? Is this person a bottom-line person, or is quality more important to him or her? Knowing what the other person values helps you emphasize that aspect of your proposal.

 It is also important to determine the person's level of authority. If the person is going to have to get approval from folks several rungs up the organizational ladder, you know you'd better provide some written materials or your proposal probably won't be repeated accurately.

Prepare about the marketplace

Research your industry. It's as simple as that. A car dealer knows best about cars. A chemist knows best about chemistry. An art dealer knows best about art. If you're going to negotiate in a world that isn't familiar to you, research it. Know the players, know whom to talk to, study the terminology. Do whatever it takes to be the smartest guy or gal in the room.

You should definitely have your personal evaluation of everything being negotiated. You should also have a good idea of how the other party values whatever is being negotiated. Don't be afraid to ask questions. You can even ask such questions of the person you are negotiating with. Asking questions shows the other party that you're interested and willing to learn.

Be a constant student of the industry or business in which you work. People who have a spent a lifetime with a company bring added value to the company simply because of all the information they have stored in their heads. The more you know about the business environment in general and your company in particular, the better off you are.

Set goals and limits

The only way to achieve anything is to set goals. Sometimes your goal setting can be quite subconscious. This triggers the impulse purchase. You see something you want, you set your goal to acquire it, your hand goes out, you grab it, and it's yours. That is a familiar retail scenario. In the business situation, setting goals is a more-serious, labor-intensive process.

When setting goals, you need to have a brainstorming session where all the possibilities are explored for any given negotiation. Then you have to pare back your list so you have a manageable number of goals to work on. You don't want to overload any single negotiation with all your hopes and dreams for all times. Go into a negotiation with an appropriate list of things to achieve.

Before starting your next negotiation, ask yourself this simple question: "What do I want out of this negotiation?" Don't be afraid to answer it. Talk it out. The easiest and fastest way to keep your goals in mind is to write them down. This helps you visualize them and makes them real.

After you've nailed down your goals, you need to set limits. Setting your limits simply means to determine the point at which you are willing to walk away from this deal and close the deal elsewhere. For instance, you set limits when you interview for a job by establishing the lowest salary you'll accept.

Setting limits is a scary thing. It takes practice for some people, but if you don't do it, others will take and take and take as long as you keep giving. At some point, you'll realize that you have given too much — a line has been crossed — all because you did not set your limits ahead of time. If you find this happening to you, read Chapter 2 for three steps to setting limits.

Listen

The vast majority of people think they are good listeners. Instead of gratifying your ego with self-indulgent reassurance, find out the true state of your listening skills from objective evidence or those who will be brutally honest with you.

Learning to listen is one of the most important skills to develop when negotiating. Before a negotiation, know the specific areas where you want to gather information. Listen attentively during the meeting. Get the most information you can, and you will have a successful negotiation.

Check your bad listening habits at the door. Always expect to find *something* of value from the other person. The rewards of good listening skills are amazing. I cover ways to improve your listening skills and give you a few tips to be sure that nothing stands in the way of you and good listening in Chapter 4.

Stated affirmatively, here are some tips for becoming a good listener:

- ✔ Count to three before responding to a question so that the question (or comment) can sink in.
- ✔ Keep notes. Be sure that you are fully awake and present.

If you experience communication problems during a negotiation, it's probably because you or the other party wasn't listening.

Part of the listening process involves interaction between the two parties. Don't be afraid to ask questions as you gather your information. When you ask questions, you refine the information you have received from the other party. Questions are a real power tool, and I cover them in Chapter 3 in detail. If you don't get the information you want to receive, ask a follow-up question. And never, ever interrupt someone who is trying to answer a question you have asked.

Whatever you do, don't accept any substitutes for the information you're seeking. Some folks will try to dodge a question or make a strong general statement instead of answering your specific question. If someone responds to your question without answering it, ask it a little differently. But don't let them off the hook.

Be clear

When I say be clear, I mean be clear in what you say and what you do. This sounds easier than it is. You must be sure that your actions, your body language, your tone of voice, and your words all send the same message.

Tips for being clear include

- ✔ Know your purpose in speaking and cut the mumbo-jumbo.
- ✔ Keep all your commitments. If you say that you are going to get back to someone at 10 a.m., be sure that you get back to them at 10 a.m. In the rush of the workday, we often short-change ourselves and others on clarity. When you say one thing and do another, you may confuse people.

Good communicators are consistent communicators.

When you become sensitive to being clear, you can start help-ing others. You can tactfully bring the tangent people back to the point of the conversation and subtly curb the inter-rupters. When you meet people who are unprepared, you can educate them and bring them up to speed. You can get some pointers on improving your clarity, as well as other's clarity, in Chapter 5. As you master the six skills, you model them for others on your team and often to those on the other side of the table. And the negotiation goes all the better for it.

Push the pause button

Everyone has a *pause button* — a little device inside your head that helps you maintain emotional distance in a negotiation. Some people use it more than others. Others don't use it all. The pause button can take many forms — it can be a break during a heated negotiation, or it can be a moment of silence when you don't agree with someone's argument.

When you use your pause button during a negotiation, you prevent yourself from saying things you may later regret. Your pause button also allows you a moment of reflection. When you don't use your pause button, you may jump into a deal too quickly because you didn't spend enough time think-ing about your words and actions.

Never let your emotions take control of your actions. Figure out in advance what sets you off. Identify your hot buttons. When you know what upsets you, talk about it with others on your team so you and they are ready if this kind of situa-tion arises. We all have hot buttons, so we may as well deal with them upfront. I talk more about the benefits of using the pause button and ways to cool your hot buttons in Chapter 6.

If a negotiation looks to be headed south and talks are at a standstill, don't panic. Use your pause button. Think about the steps that got you to this point. Instead of making outland-ish demands or angrily storming out of the negotiating room, take a breather and suggest meeting at a later time.

Closing the deal

Sometimes deals don't seem to close even when the parties are more or less in agreement on all the important issues. Sometimes this happens because someone in the room is being difficult. Maybe a person is being a bully or trying to pull the wool over your eyes. Maybe someone is disrupting the proceedings by yelling or being bossy. Pushing past these problems involves pushing the pause button — hard. Take breaks as often as necessary so everyone has a chance to regroup. Keep in mind that you're not the only person in the room affected by these people.

Sometime deals get hung up because of the other side's tactics. You probably can list them as well as anyone: a constant change of position, playing good cop/bad cop, having to check with an invisible partner. When you run into one of these behaviors, push the pause button. When you're on a break, analyze your opponent's tactics, and when you return to the negotiating table, ask specific questions of the other side. Listen carefully to get around the obstruction.

Closing is the culmination of the negotiation process, which I focus on in Chapter 7. It's the point where everything comes together, when two parties mutually agree on the terms of the deal. But how soon is too soon to close? The answer: It's never too soon to close. You want to start closing as quickly and efficiently as possible — under reasonable parameters, of course. You don't have to close the whole deal right away. You can close a piece of it by agreeing tentatively and moving on to other issues.

Closing the deal isn't always a smooth process. Sometimes you are dealing with someone who fears making a bad deal or is afraid of his or her boss who never likes a result no matter how good it is and how hard everyone worked. Again, ask a lot of questions to find out what is going on, and then help this person with his or her problem.

A good negotiator is often just someone who helps the other side understand all the good points of his or her proposal and gives the other person the tools and arguments to sell the proposal to whoever needs to be sold.

The six negotiating skills in one film

Dog Day Afternoon is probably the best single film on negotiating that you can watch. Millions have seen a very young Al Pacino and Charles Durning turn in virtuoso performances as captor and cop in this classic film. Based on the true story of a bank robbery that turned into a hostage situation, the film shows the local police team trying hard to resolve the situation but fumbling a bit. Then the FBI team moves quickly into action and negotiates with skill and training. The events were re-created with incredible accuracy.

Each of the six basic principles of negotiating is clearly demonstrated in this film:

✔ **Prepare:** You'll notice right away that the robbers are unprepared for the hostage situation. They came to rob a bank, not to take hostages. In fact, one of the team members bails out immediately in a comic lesson about the importance of building a solid team that is fully prepared. Note how the police immediately and throughout the film try to gather information about the man holding the hostages. They use all the resources of the state to find out who they are negotiating against. Within hours, the cops find out things that shocked the man's mother and his wife.

✔ **Set goals and limits:** The police set limits before they ever start talking. Their goal is to get the hostages out safely. When a hostage is hurt, they find out how the injury happened. If it was an accident, they continue the negotiation. If it was an execution, they make a frontal assault on the site. Through it all, they never forget their goal, even though they appear willing to do so as far as the captors know.

✔ **Listen and clarify communications:** This is a constant. Note in the barber shop that someone is always in the background wearing headphones. That officer is monitoring all the communications both ways to be sure that they are clear. He does not speak, but he is an integral member of the negotiating team. Also, note the body language of the FBI agent when he first meets Pacino's character. The agent conveys authority and confidence, unlike the local policemen.

✔ **Push the pause button:** One officer's sole job is to observe everyone's emotional state. This officer keeps a check on emotions and removes officers before the strain of the situation overcomes them.

✔ **Close:** The authorities keep the goal constantly in mind. Notice how many times the police try to close this negotiation.

Dog Day Afternoon is so instructive that it is shown at the FBI training school for hostage negotiators in Quantico, Virginia.

Handling All Sorts of Negotiations

You can apply the six basic skills to every negotiation, no matter what. But some of the negotiations you'll encounter may seem beyond the scope of these skills. Trust me, they aren't. You simply have to remain focused on the six skills.

Negotiations can become complex for any number of reasons, and male-female negotiations often have an element of complexity to them. And as the world seems to grow smaller and move faster, you're likely to face international negotiations and negotiations that take place over the telephone and Internet.

When negotiations get complicated

In simple negotiations, you can apply the six basic skills without too much trouble. But what happens when a negotiation gets complicated? Complex negotiations happen when the negotiation becomes larger in scope, and the amount of work and organization requires more than two people (one on each side of the negotiating table) can handle alone. When the negotiation shifts from a two-person affair to a 20-person affair, the negotiation is complicated. On a personal level, a negotiation becomes complicated when you invest all your emotion and effort into getting the deal closed. For example, a salary negotiation, although simple in theory, carries a lot of emotional weight behind it.

No matter the size and factors involved in the negotiation, the six basic skills serve as your core to making the negotiation a success.

Gender differences in negotiating

Although I hate to generalize, some generalizations are both appropriate and necessary when it comes to differing negotiating styles between men and women:

> ✔ Men think in linear terms, going from A to B to C to D, and then, if you're lucky, begin to expand from there. Men love logic and want a rational explanation for any solution that is offered.

✔ Women start with the big picture and then focus in on the details. They tend to be much more confident of their intuition.

Although these generalizations may not apply to you in particular, you need to be aware of how differently most men and women communicate at work. Even if you think you don't fit the typical mold for your gender, you will negotiate with men and women who do.

Women and men can learn from each other. Respect the differences and alter your style to be heard. You can be the world's best negotiator, but if your words are not heard, your message doesn't matter.

Four strategies for women who want men to hear them

Women have been socialized to avoid verbal confrontation more than men and to speak more politely. The following list contains strategies for women who want men to hear them:

✔ **Avoid apologies.** Women tend to apologize more than men. Even assertive women sometimes unwittingly use power-robbing devices, including the following:

• Prefacing and tagging: *Prefacing* is leading into a statement with a phrase that weakens it. For example, "I'm not sure about this, but . . ." *Tagging* is adding a qualifying phrase at the end of a statement. For example, "We should take action, don't you think?" "Don't you think" and "Am I right?" are common tags that weaken a statement.

• A *questioning tone* is an intonation that goes up a little at the end of a sentence. This tone takes the power right out of an otherwise declarative sentence and makes the speaker sound as if she's unsure and lacks self-confidence.

• *Hedges* or *qualifiers* such as "kind of" and "sort of" they steal power from women's statements. These *unsure words* are weak and make *you* seem weak.

• *Nonwords* are all those little extras that get plugged into speech — those words or sounds that replace silence and give you a pause to pull together your next thought. Instead of *umm* and *er,* use the silence to give power to your statements and opinions.

✔ **Be brief.** Women use talk to build relationships, so they tell stories. Men use talk to exchange information, so they swap facts.

Women generally use more details in their conversations than men. The information you want the male listener to hear may be lost in all those details. During a negotiation, watch for signs that a male listener is glazing over and cut down on the number of words immediately. In fact, tell men right at the start how long the story will take and stay within the allotted time.

✔ **Be direct; don't hint.** Make sure that you are direct — even to the point of spelling something out. Men, more so than women, require clear messages as well as brief ones.

✔ **Avoid emotional displays.** Crying or other emotional displays in a negotiation can be more distracting than a low-cut dress, and an outburst can be just as ruinous to a woman's position in a negotiation.

If you feel a cry coming on, excuse yourself, go to the bathroom, and cry your eyes out. When you're finished, check your makeup, take a deep breath, and go back to the meeting.

Four strategies for men who want women to hear them

Some speech mannerisms, common among men, are so off-putting to women that they rob men of the opportunity to be heard no matter how valuable the words are. The following list contains strategies for men who want women to hear them:

✔ **Don't be condescending.** Don't refer to someone as "honey," "baby," "sweetie," or with other malapropisms. For a man to use these phrases when talking to a co-worker is inappropriate because they say that you don't see a woman as a valuable team member, a contributing co-worker, or an important team member. You see her in her personal role, just as you would a woman you were trying to pick up at happy hour.

Respect everyone you work with if you want them to respect you and do their best for you. When your words flow from a place of respect, they don't contain such verbal pats on the head.

✔ **Share before deciding.** The natural way for a man to express his conclusions is at the very end of the process — to announce his decision after he makes it. But if you're totally silent during the decision-making process, a woman may think you are shut down. It may be hard for her to stay interested, and she may become frustrated with the lack of feedback.

✔ **Share something personal.** This is not a suggestion to be intrusive or sexual; it's a suggestion to show your humanity. Studies show that one of women's biggest frustrations with men is their failure to open up. Nothing shows openness better than sharing something about your family, background, or personal history.

A man needs to be very careful when complimenting a woman in the workplace. A beautiful fountain pen or an attractive briefcase are safe areas for compliments. Dresses and perfumes are dangerous. Necklaces and necklines are absolutely never appropriate topics for comment. The smart advice is "When in doubt, don't."

✔ **Avoid emotional displays.** Yelling and other emotional displays can ruin a man's position in a negotiation. Many men still think yelling when they are frustrated or angry is acceptable behavior. Men and women feel that a man who yells is being dominating and controlling.

If you feel a yell coming on, excuse yourself, get away from people, and yell your lungs out. When you're finished, splash some water on your face, take a deep breath, and go back to the meeting.

International negotiations

International negotiation (or cross-cultural negotiation) is one of many specialized areas in the world of negotiating. The six basic skills are just as critical, if not more critical, in international negotiations as they are when you're negotiating on home turf. International deals require more preparation because you have to tailor your negotiating approach to the customs of the country you're negotiating in.

Preparing for cross-cultural negotiating requires more than just understanding how foreigners close a deal. You have to know the differences in communication, their attitude toward conflict, how they complete tasks, their decision-making processes, and how they disclose information. Even the body language in other countries is very different from what we're accustomed to in the United States. Eye contact, personal space, and touch vary among countries.

Research the country's traditions before walking into a negotiating room on foreign soil. Watch foreign language films, read travel guides, and learn key phrases in your counterpart's language during the preparation process. Bridge the communication gap as much as possible. When you start behaving like a native, you'll earn the respect and confidence of your foreign counterpart.

Negotiation on the phone and via the Internet

We're riding on the information superhighway and never looking back. The landscape of communication has changed dramatically, thanks to the telephone and the Internet. These forms of telecommunication have made communication faster and sometimes simpler. More importantly, they've created a new mode of negotiating. You can now negotiate from the comfort of your own home, in a car while driving to your office, or from a different part of the world.

Negotiating via the telephone and Internet requires the same preparation and etiquette as a face-to-face negotiation. The only difference is that the negotiation happens at the lift of a headset or the push of a button. Although simpler, using the telephone or Internet to negotiate is not as good as negotiating in person. You miss the human interaction, the body language, and the gestures that are so important in gauging others when negotiating in a room. For more on telephone and Internet-based negotiations, see Chapter 9.

Chapter 2

Setting and Enforcing Limits

• •

In This Chapter

▶ Discovering the advantages of setting limits

▶ Setting limits for yourself

▶ Holding yourself to your limits

▶ Walking away from a negotiation

• •

*S*etting limits and then sticking to them is one of the most important and most difficult lessons you can learn. This chapter tells you how to set limits and then how to use those limits to take charge of every negotiation in your personal and professional life.

If you're like most people, you can use some pointers about limits. To help you conquer this nearly universal problem, I divide it into two pieces. One is setting your limits. The other is enforcing your limits.

Set your limits before you enter a negotiation. Setting limits early saves an enormous amount of time during the actual course of the negotiation because you already know your options. And knowing your options makes you more decisive during the discussions.

When you carefully and realistically predetermine your limits, they serve as rudders, navigating the negotiation through rough waters. Worried about dirty tricks being thrown at you? Scared of unfair tactics? No worries, as long as you set your limits.

What It Means to Set Limits

Your limits define the absolute most you are willing to give up to get what you want. Setting limits means establishing the point at which you are willing to walk away from the negotiation and pursue some alternative course.

Your limit may be the highest price you'll pay for a product, the lowest salary you'll accept from a prospective employer, the maximum number of days you're willing to travel for your job. If the negotiation doesn't close before your limits are crossed, then there's no deal.

In business negotiations, setting limits may not seem necessary because the marketplace can define the boundaries of the discussion. People generally have an idea about the price of goods or services; they know what others are paying. They assume the discussion will not go beyond an acceptable range or what they consider to be a fair and reasonable value for the product or service under negotiation. But even business negotiations can go off track, especially in times of economic downturn or if other business conditions change suddenly.

Setting limits is worth the effort. People who consistently make bad deals usually don't set limits before the negotiation starts and don't know when to walk away. Knowing that you're prepared to walk away gives you the strength and confidence to be firm, even if the other party isn't aware of your limits or your ability to enforce them.

Setting Limits in Three Easy Steps

When you know how to set limits and have confidence in that ability, you change the entire negotiating process. But it is almost impossible to set and enforce limits unless you have an attitude of prosperity. People who believe that the world is a stingy place and see the world through an attitude of lack and limitation usually think that they *have to* close the deal or another one won't come their way. The truth is that the universe is a bountiful place. No matter what your calling, there are more jobs, more opportunities, more chances to express your success than you could ever possibly take advantage of. Embrace the magnificent range of possibilities that life has to offer as you read this section because that is the mind-set of a world-class negotiator.

This section contains three steps that master negotiators around the world use to set limits. Notice how each of these steps includes the word "know."

Know that you have other choices

Poor negotiators tend to attach themselves to the notion that they must close every negotiation with a purchase or sale. Good negotiators, on the other hand, often walk away. Walking away from a bad deal is just as important — maybe more important — than closing a good deal. (For more on walking away, see the last section of the chapter, "Sometimes, the Best Deal in Town Is No Deal at All.")

In fact, you often have two incentives to walk away from a bad deal:

- ✔ You aren't stuck with the headache, financial stress, or other difficulties associated with the bad deal.
- ✔ One of your competitors will end up with the job, while you are off chasing the good job, the profitable job, the job with the clients who are easy to work with.

"There is always another deal around the corner." Make this phrase your mantra. Repeat it until it becomes part of your core. Own it. This truth can influence your entire life and bring positive results to all your future negotiations. Another deal is always waiting for you somewhere. It just may take some time to find it.

Know what the other choices are

Don't develop just one alternative deal in a negotiation. List all the alternatives available to you should the negotiation fail to close on the terms you want. You have nothing to lose and everything to gain by listing your choices. List all your options, even if you don't think they're very valuable or practical. You have plenty of time to edit them later. Life is always about exercising options.

If you're interviewing for a job, your alternatives may involve accepting a lower wage, accepting another job, continuing your search, going to another city, changing professions, or going into business for yourself. The point is that you have many alternatives. Don't limit yourself.

If you find that you can't list any alternatives, you aren't ready to start negotiating. One result of being well prepared is the ability to create this list of alternatives before a negotiation begins.

Before you enter the negotiation, try constructing a similar list of alternatives for the other party. The more you know about the choices available to the other side, the more strength you have in the negotiation. Consider these exercises as a part of your preparation.

Know your "or else"

After you have created the list of alternatives, decide which alternative is most acceptable to you. Pick your personal *or else*. Decide what you want to do if the negotiation doesn't close. Think about that course of action. Play the scenario out in your mind.

Knowing what your "or else" is — that is, knowing what your favorite option is if the deal doesn't close — defines your limits for each negotiation. Suppose that you're willing to pay $300,000 for a house before you set your "or else." Then remind yourself that you have choices and list all of them. After you write down your list, you may decide that you can accept another house that's cheaper. This way, you can be firm or even lower the price you were willing to offer. On the other hand, if you decide that no other house would be right for you, the price could go up rather than down.

Most negotiations settle before either party's limits are tested. World-class negotiators have been doing this for centuries. Your limits and the other party's limits loom over every negotiation. You are much better accepting this reality before the negotiation ever starts.

Enforcing Your Limits

It goes without saying that you can't enforce limits if you don't have them. In personal relationships, people often don't express limits until they are crossed. When raising children, parents often express limits as rules — rules that must be followed or there will be consequences. This model often helps people who think they have a hard time setting and enforcing limits.

The next four sections help you enforce your limits. No one else will do this for you.

Write down your limits

When you write down your limits — your walk-away points — before you start negotiating, you are well on your way to remembering — and enforcing — your limits. Unless you write down your "or else," you may forget it in the excitement of the negotiation. It's easy to get caught up and reach an agreement you wouldn't otherwise agree to you had set your limits and then remembered them as the negotiation drew to a close.

Establish your resistance point

One reason you must be very certain to set limits is that they automatically define your resistance point. Your *resistance point* is close to your limit but leaves enough room to close the deal without crossing your limit. At the resistance point, you let the other party know that he or she is getting close to your limit — and that you will soon be walking away. Resist any proposal that too closely approaches the limits you set.

Don't remain silent until the other party crosses the limit. Your counterpart needs to hear that the negotiation is approaching a resistance point before the discussion reaches a critical point. You can bet that the other party will be hurt and angry when you walk out if he or she hasn't had a clear warning from you in advance.

How far out in front of the limit you set your resistance point is a matter of your own personality and comfort zone.

Tell your team the limits

Obviously, you don't go into a negotiation and announce your bottom line, such as the most you're willing to pay. But you do need to tell your teammates about the limit you have set (and remind them not to let those specifics slip to the opposing side). Just as important, make sure that everyone understands that you (or someone else) haven't just pulled an arbitrary figure out of the air. Your team needs to know and agree with with limit set.

By the same token, don't be afraid to make adjustments if someone on your team makes a compelling argument to change the limit before the negotiation starts. Also, if — and only if — you gain new information during the negotiation, you can adjust your limit. However, don't fall into the trap of "having" to close the deal. If the other side isn't willing to settle within your acceptable range, find someone who will.

Never paint yourself into a corner

If you state your limits immediately when negotiations begin, you violate a fundamental tenet of sound negotiations: Never, ever paint yourself into a corner. In negotiations, you paint yourself into a corner by taking a strong stand and not leaving yourself an alternative, or an *out*.

In other words, don't start a negotiation by telling someone that you won't pay one dime more than 50 bucks (or whatever) unless you know that other stores offer the same product within your price range. Such an announcement paints you into a corner when no alternative exists.

Practicing Negotiating toward a Limit

Limits are not much help if you cave in every time you set them. In the beginning, practice the steps in situations outside of your business relationships. It is particularly fun and somewhat easier, psychologically, to walk away from a deal when you're on vacation. You are browsing at your leisure, and you see something you want to buy. Be sure that you are willing to buy the item, because you may just close the deal. Be equally sure that you are willing to leave the shop without the item, because that is the point of this game.

Note the price. Determine what you are willing to pay for it, which must be much less than the indicated price. When you have set a price, begin talking with the shopkeeper. Don't say what your bottom-line price is. Instead, offer less than you are willing to pay but above what you think the shopkeeper paid.

Don't just grab a number because you want to play a game with the shopkeeper. Give serious thought to the true value of the item.

If no further negotiation takes place, say thanks and politely walk out. Closing even this non-negotiation in a formal way is important. You offered the shopkeeper an opportunity to move some merchandise. Make sure that the shopkeeper knows the opportunity is passing.

The shopkeeper may well respond with a lower offer. Don't automatically accept. Remember that, although you are willing to purchase the item, you are seeking the experience of hanging tough, even walking away from a deal. You may increase your offer slightly but don't move too fast toward the end point. After all, you want to practice!

If the shopkeeper quickly meets your unstated limit, keep the negotiation going. Adjust your price downward, toward your last stated position. When a buyer with cash meets a willing seller, what follows may surprise you even in shops where you think bargaining is strictly forbidden.

How to Tell the Other Party When You're the One Walking Away

If you decide (based on your solid preparation and honest judgment) to terminate a negotiation, don't send a conflicting message. State clearly the conditions under which negotiations can resume. Then walk. Don't look back or otherwise communicate hesitation.

Never terminate a negotiation when you are angry. Before you walk away from a negotiation, give yourself some breathing room. If, after some thought, you want to terminate the negotiations, end the discussion in a way that doesn't damage your reputation in the community — whether the community is your firm, your industry, or your city. Do it in a way that allows you to do business with those who like or respect your current counterpart.

Before you walk away from the negotiation, write a wrap-up letter. Writing a letter gives you time to edit and correct yourself. It clarifies your view of the situation and puts things in perspective in case the other side is mistaken about some aspect of the situation. Your letter should cover each of the following:

1. **Summarize the final position of the other side.**

   Be painfully accurate. Introduce this section with hedge words, such as "To the best of my memory . . . " or "If I understood you correctly. . . ." Close this section with "If that does not correctly state your position, please advise." Such phrases enable the other side to change position or make a correction without losing face or being argumentative.

2. **Summarize your own position.**

   Be painfully accurate. Here again, hedge words let the other side reenter gracefully. Examples include: "In case it was not clear during our discussions . . . ," or "I'm sorry if this was not presented as clearly in our discussions as it is in this letter."

3. **Explain about square pegs in round holes.**

   If you simply don't believe that a deal can be made because the needs and desires are so different, say so. No one is blameworthy. The parties can work together on another project when the fit is better.

4. **Never, ever blame the other person.**

   Even if you are walking away because you have decided the other person is a sleazebag, hog breath, scumbag, you won't gain anything by putting that assessment in writing. The sleazebag may have a sister-in-law or cousin whom you may want to do business with in the future. Never burn a bridge — a bridge serves an entire village, not just one person.

5. **Include a message of thanks.**

   Always include in your letter a thank-you sentence for the time and attention you did receive. This final touch is the classy thing to do.

6. **Telegraph your next move.**

   This feature is optional. A sentence such as "We will try to sell the item elsewhere," or "Next spring, we will try such a launch again" tells the other side that you have other options, and you will be exercising them. Of course, the sensitivity of the situation may limit you to a statement such as "We will be moving on," or "We will be examining our options over the next few weeks."

The Consequences of Not Setting Limits

Even if you haven't consciously set limits, you have a point beyond which you won't go in every negotiation. There's also a point beyond which your opponent won't go. If you don't set your limits ahead of time, you discover them as your patience becomes strained. Often, people explode or feel stepped on when this line is crossed.

Much of setting limits is really figuring out what your limits are — before they come up and hit you in the face because someone crossed them.

If a negotiation terminates because demands crossed the limits of one party or the other, the end happens as swiftly, silently, and unexpectedly as a pigeon hit from behind by a diving predator. The surprise factor is stunning. Usually, one or both parties feel betrayed or angry or both. In truth, setting your limits in advance can completely avoid the problem. Each party is aware of the limits that form the negotiating boundaries.

Re-examining Your Limits

Set your *bottom line* (that is, the point beyond which you will not go) before you ever start negotiating. In fact, set a bottom line as soon as you have the data to do so. But don't be afraid to take a second look at the limits you set.

When you have set your limits, write them down. Writing them down doesn't mean that they won't change, but having a written record does mean that you can't fudge later and pretend that you aren't adjusting limits. During the heat of the negotiation, you don't need to panic when your limits are tested because you have them written down in front of you.

Slowly changing limits during a negotiation without mindful consideration is a very common mistake. If you are conscious of what you're doing and keenly aware of the reasons, changing limits can be a positive and appropriate course of action. However, if you don't write down your limits — your "or else" — you risk adjusting them by inches when a foot is needed. Slipping and sliding creates confusion in your mind and in the minds of those with whom you are negotiating.

Sometimes, the Best Deal in Town Is No Deal at All

Setting limits is tough. Walking away is even tougher. You may actually be afraid that something bad is going to happen if you walk away from a negotiation. Walking away often feels like failure. Don't worry — nothing terrible will occur if you walk away. Life goes on.

You can find out much about negotiation by walking away from a deal or two just for the practice. It's okay, and it can be educational.

Knowing how to walk away is critically important in your personal negotiations. How many people do you know who are miserable because they don't have the strength or the experience to set limits in the workplace or at home with children or spouses? People stay in bad relationships longer than is healthy because of their inability to set limits and stick to them.

Chapter 3

Asking the Right Questions

. . . .

In This Chapter

▶ Developing the ability to ask good questions

▶ Avoiding the pitfalls of questioning

▶ Getting the information you need

▶ Making sure people are listening

. . . .

*H*ow you ask questions during a negotiation is very important because questions open the door to knowledge — knowledge about the other party and knowledge about the negotiation at hand. Questions are the keys to the kingdom. No one ever wasted time asking a smart question.

This chapter covers the art of effective questioning during a negotiation. Asking appropriate questions, knowing when to ask those questions, and knowing when *not* to ask those questions are all techniques you should master. They will lead you to a path of negotiating success. And even if a negotiation is at a standstill, knowing how to ask the right questions creates a discussion between you and the other party. That can lead to positive results if your information is funneled wisely.

Tickle It Out: The Art of Coaxing Out Information

Effective listening requires probing. No one says everything you want to hear in the exact order, depth, and detail that you prefer. You have to ask. No phrase describes the job of questioning better than *tickle it out*. Questions are a way of coaxing out information that you want or need. Developing the ability to ask good questions is a lifelong effort.

In a trial, the question-and-answer format rules the proceedings. Attorneys and the judge can talk to each other in declarative sentences, but all the testimony is presented in the somewhat artificial format of question-and-answer. In court, the purpose of every question should be to obtain specific information. If the question isn't answered directly, it needs to be asked in another way. The rules in the courtroom are pretty specific; as a matter of etiquette, you should apply similar rules in a business meeting. For example, courtesy prohibits you from barraging the other side with rapid-fire questions; court rules prevent the same thing.

Battling the jargon

Don't be shy or embarrassed about asking someone to clarify a statement. Many people use jargon or shorthand when they talk, so you can't always be sure of what they mean, particularly if you and the person you're negotiating with work in different industries. You just need to ask for clarification.

A slightly more difficult situation arises when you are both in the same industry, and the other person assumes that you know the meaning of words that he or she is using. You may feel embarrassed to ask for the meaning under that circumstance, because you think that you *should* know. You can handle this situation by saying, "Just to be sure that we're using the same shorthand, tell me exactly how you define XYZ." When the other person gives you his or her definition, use it. Here are three useful responses when the other party defines a term for you:

- ✔ "That's great! We use that phrase the same way."

- ✔ "Glad I asked; we use that phrase a little differently, but we can go with your definition."

- ✔ "Thanks, I just learned something new."

If you think misunderstandings are likely if you use a term your opponent's way instead of your way, say: "We should define that term in the written agreement so others won't get confused. You and I know what we're talking about, but we want to be sure that everyone else does, too." Don't get into a battle over definitions.

Clarifying relativity

Requiring others to define relative words is just as important as asking them to explain specific pieces of jargon. *Relative words* are nonspecific, descriptive words that only have meaning in relation to something else. Some relative words that can create a great deal of confusion include

- Cheap
- High quality
- Large
- Many
- Soon
- Substantial

Don't be shy about asking for clarification when someone uses one of these words. If the person insists on using generalities, as some people do, press for a range. If you still don't get a specific answer, supply two or three ranges and force the person to choose one.

A new customer says, "We're thinking of placing a big order with you." That's good news if you and your new customer both use the words "big order" the same way. But you need to ask for specifics: "Do you mean more like ten, or maybe about a hundred, or would it be closer to a thousand?" Whatever the answer is, just say "thank you." Don't belabor the point that you wouldn't call that a "big order."

These situations offer a great opportunity to find out more about the company you're dealing with. It's a good time to ask questions about the normal size of the orders from this company, why it's changing now, and other pieces of information that will help you service this client much better.

Asking Good Questions: A Real Power Tool

When you listen attentively, you make an incredible discovery. Sometimes, the person is not delivering the information you need. The chief tool of the good listener is a good question. Questions are marvelous tools for stimulating, drawing out, and guiding communication.

Asking a good question is a learned skill requiring years of training. The foundation of good question-asking is knowing what information you want to obtain. Use these seven handy guidelines for asking better questions:

- ✔ **Plan your questions in advance.** Prepare what you're going to ask about but don't memorize the exact wording, or you'll sound artificial. It pays to outline your purpose and a sequence of related questions so that you can follow the speaker's train of thought. Pretty soon, the speaker is comfortably divulging information. The question-and-answer format can act as an aid to good communication rather than a block.

- ✔ **Ask with a purpose.** Every question you ask should have one of two basic purposes: to get facts or to get opinions (see Table 3-1 for examples of each). Know which is your goal and go for it, but don't confuse the two concepts.

- ✔ **Tailor your question to your listener.** Relate questions to the listener's frame of reference and background. Be sure to use words and phrases the listener understands. Don't use computer jargon with your technologically handicapped boss.

- ✔ **Follow general questions with more specific ones.** These specific inquiries, called *follow-up questions,* generally get you past the fluff and into more of the meat-and-potatoes information. This progression is also the way that most people think, so you are leading them down a natural path. The follow-up question is the one that ferrets out the facts.

- ✔ **Keep questions short and clear — cover only one subject.** Questions are just a way to lead people into telling you what you want to know. Crafting short questions takes more energy, but the effort is worth it. If you really want to know two different things, ask two different questions. You're the one who wants the information; you're the one who should do the work. Pretty soon, the other party is talking to you about the subject, and you can drop the questioning all together.

✔ **Make transitions between their answers and your questions.** Listen to the answer to your first question. Use something in the answer to frame your next question. Even if this takes you off the path for a while, it leads to rich rewards because of the comfort level it provides to the person you're questioning. This approach also sounds more conversational and therefore less threatening.

✔ **Don't interrupt; let the other person answer the question!** You're asking the questions to get answers, so it almost goes without saying that you need to stop talking and listen.

Table 3-1   The Two Goals of Asking Questions

To Get Facts	To Get Opinions
"When did you begin work on the plan?"	"How good is this plan?"
"How many employees are available?"	"Will the schedule work?"
"What are the dimensions of the house?"	"What do you think of the design?"
"Which car reached the intersection first?"	"Who caused the accident?"

Avoid intimidation

A sharp negotiator who is trying to sell you something may try to use a series of questions, each one designed to elicit a "yes" response. This sequence of questions leads to a final query posed in the same manner. When you respond in the affirmative to this final question, the negotiation is complete — and you have agreed to your counterpart's terms.

That technique may work for a negotiation with someone you never plan to see again. It doesn't work so well with people whom you plan to have a long-term relationship with. You want the other party to understand and agree with the outcome, not to be tricked into signing a piece of paper that he or she may regret later.

Learn from negotiations by asking questions

To profit from experience, you must be open and willing to learn, even from what some people may consider a failure. What appears to be a failure can actually lead to new opportunities. That's why so many companies have postmortem meetings, especially after a negotiation that did not go so well. Use open-ended questions as a starting point for the next phase of learning:

✓ What went well and why?

✓ What went less well and why?

✓ What would you do differently now?

✓ What would you do the same way?

✓ What went unexpectedly well and why?

✓ What went unexpectedly badly and why?

✓ What new assumptions/rules should be made?

✓ What additional information would have been helpful? How could you have foreseen what happened?

✓ How can you improve learning in the future?

Some people use questions to intimidate or beat up on others. Someone may ask you, "Why in the world would you want to wear a hat like that?" The best answer is often no answer. Let a few beats go by and then go on without answering or acknowledging the question. Some conduct is unworthy of any of your time or energy. Keep your eye on your own goal and ignore the diversion.

Ask, don't tell

How you ask questions is very important in establishing effective communication. Effective questions open the door to knowledge and understanding. But you must be watchful that asking questions does not evolve into you *telling* the other person instead of *asking*. You have probably heard a question like, "Isn't it true that no one has ever charged that much for a widget?" or better yet, "Can you name one company that met such a deadline?" These are statements masked as questions. You usually can detect a shift from asking to telling by the tone of voice that the person uses as he or she asks these questions. The art of questioning lies in truly wanting to acquire the information that would be contained in the answer.

Effective questioning leads to

✔ **Establishing rapport:** *Rapport* is the ability to understand and to connect with others, both mentally and emotionally. It's the ability to work with people to build a climate of trust and respect. Having rapport doesn't mean that you have to agree, but that you understand where the other person is coming from. It starts with accepting the other person's point of view and his or her style of communication.

✔ **Better listening, deeper understanding:** Oftentimes while you are talking, the other person is not listening but thinking about what he or she is going to say. When you ask questions, you engage the other person. He or she is much more likely to think about what you are saying. You lead the other person in the direction you want to take the conversation.

✔ **Higher motivation, better follow-up:** The right answer will not be imposed by your questions. It will be found and owned by the other person, who will be more motivated to follow it up. Most people are much more likely to agree with what they say than with what you say.

Avoid leading questions

To get the most telling answers and objective information, don't ask leading questions. *Leading questions* contain the germ of the answer you seek, such as

> The other person: "I've only used that golf club a couple of times."

> You: "How did you like the great weight and balance on that club?"

Because your question contains a glowing editorial of the golf club, the other person will have a difficult time saying anything negative about it, even if that's what he or she feels. A nonleading question, such as "How do you like it?" is neutral and more likely to elicit the truth — which is what you want to hear. If the other person swallows her true opinion or simply fails to express it to you because of the way you asked the question, you are the loser. She hasn't altered her feelings, she just hasn't expressed them, and you've lost an opportunity to influence her.

Table 3-2 shows leading questions and alternatives more likely to extract accurate information or honest opinions.

Table 3-2	Leading and Non-Leading Questions
Leading Questions	*More Productive Alternatives*
"Don't you think that such-and-such is true?"	"What do you think about such-and-such?"
"Isn't $10 the usual price of this item?"	"What is the usual price of this item?"
"Everyone agrees that this widget is best; don't you?"	"Which widget do you think is best?"

Leading questions don't help you improve your listening skills or get the highest quality information.

Don't assume anything

Good listening requires that you don't assume anything about the intention of the speaker. This rule is especially true in conversations with family, friends, and work associates. Your familiarity can lead you to presume that you understand a speaker's point — without carefully considering what this person is actually saying to you. Be wary of jumping to conclusions about the speaker's intent, especially with the important inner circle of people closest to you.

In business, leading questions are often viewed as improper. At a minimum, they are challenging, which often leads to hostility. Here is an example:

> "Why does your company insist on overcharging on this item?"

To break down this question so it doesn't make any assumptions, you need to ask three separate questions:

> ✔ "What does your company charge for this item?"
>
> ✔ "What do other companies charge for this item?"
>
> ✔ "Why do you think this discrepancy in pricing exists?"

You get at the truth and you eliminate the hostility.

Note that in this example you and the other person may have different pricing information. Breaking the question down offers an opportunity to clear up this difference without getting into an argument.

Ask open-ended questions

Unlike simple yes-or-no questions, *open-ended questions* invite the respondent to talk — and enable you to get much more information. These are the types of questions to use when you want to find out a person's opinion or gather some facts during the course of a negotiation. The more you get the other person to talk, the more information you learn. Yes-or-no questions (called *closed questions*) limit choices and force a decision.

A simple closed question requiring a yes-or-no answer:

"Do you like this car?"

An open-ended question, on the other hand, encourages the person to start talking:

"What do you like best about this car?"

Try classic open-ended questions when you need to get information.

Asking a question in the declarative format — "Tell me about that." — as a request rather than as a traditional question, can be very useful if you're dealing with a reluctant participant. People who won't answer questions will sometimes respond to a direct order.

Open-ended questions aren't the only types of questions you can use to get people to talk:

- ✓ **Fact-finding questions** are aimed at getting information on a particular subject. "Can you tell me the story about how you decided to bring this product to the market?"

- ✓ **Follow-up questions** are used to get more information or to elicit an opinion. "So after you do that, what would happen next?"

- ✓ **Feedback questions** are aimed at finding the difference that makes the difference. "May I say that back to you so I understand the difference between what you are proposing and what I was offering to do?"

Ask again

When a speaker fails to answer your question, you have two choices, depending on the situation:

- ✓ **Stop everything until you get your answer or a clear acknowledgment that your question will not be answered.** Silence can be golden at these opportunities. Most people are uncomfortable with silence. An individual may feel compelled to answer a difficult question if you remain silent after posing the question. "The next one who speaks loses."

- ✓ **Bide your time and ask the question later.** If the question was worth asking in the first place, it's worth asking again.

Which of these two techniques you use depends on the situation. If the situation is fast paced and the information you requested is fundamental to decision making, use the first technique. You can choose to bide your time whenever you know that you'll have another opportunity to get the information, and you don't need the information right away. Biding your time is always easier and less confrontational, but if you really need a piece of data, don't be afraid to say, "Wait, I need to know. . . ."

A good way to handle someone who doesn't answer your question is to make a little joke out of the situation with a statement such as, "I need to catch up." No matter how serious the subject matter of the negotiation, a little humor never hurts, especially if you use yourself as a subject of that humor.

If the person makes a little joke back to avoid the question, you may have to shift back to a serious mode. Persevere until you either get an answer to your question or you realize that you must go elsewhere. If the other party isn't going to answer your question, make a note of that fact so you remember to use other resources to get the answer you need.

Use your asks wisely

If you're lucky, the opposing side will answer most of your questions before you ask them. Have patience. Only ask essential questions. If you don't care about the answer one way or the other, don't ask. You are granted only so many *asks* in any conversation. Don't use them indiscriminately.

The consequences to asking too many questions may be that the listener becomes oversensitive to your probing, which often translates into resistance to answering your queries. When someone becomes resistant in one area, they will be resistant in other areas and, therefore, unreceptive to your general position. That's a high price to pay for asking too many questions.

To become a really good questioner, take some time after a negotiating session to think about the questions you asked. Identify the extraneous questions. Remember that every question should serve a purpose. You're not looking for damage that was done in that particular negotiation; you're evaluating the quality of the questions.

Accept no substitutes

You're actively listening (see Chapter 4 for listening tips). You're asking all the right questions at the right time. You're patient. So why aren't you getting the information you need? One of the following possibilities may exist:

- ✔ **The person simply doesn't understand your questions.** Try rephrasing them.

- ✔ **The person simply doesn't want to answer your questions.** Maybe company policy prevents disclosure of the information. Maybe the person feels uncomfortable discussing a particular subject matter. If you believe this is true, make a note and find out the information elsewhere.

✔ **The person is not good at answering questions.** The avoidance is not deliberate or devious. Because of bad habits, sloppiness, or laziness, the person neglects to respond to your inquiry. Keep probing.

✔ **The person doesn't know the answer and is uncomfortable saying so.** If you suspect this, ask if the other person needs time to research the answer.

✔ **The person is a pathological liar.** In this case, run. Never negotiate with a liar — you can't win.

In each of these cases, the result is the same. You are not getting a valuable piece of information. Take the suggested possibilities to get the information you need. Don't give up.

Dealing with Unacceptable Responses

The next three sections discuss techniques people use to avoid providing accurate answers. Do not allow these ploys. When you're alert to these substitutes for honest information, you can demand the real McCoy.

Don't tolerate the dodge

Politicians, as a group, seem specially trained to provide anything but an answer when asked a question. It's almost as though there is some secret college for Congress members where they go to learn about the artful dodge. For example, if someone asks about the state of public education, the representative may launch into a dissertation about family values. It's odd how many interviewers let elected officials get away with avoiding questions Sunday after Sunday.

You don't have to do that. Don't accept the dodge when you ask a question. Recognize this tactic for what it is and repeat the question, this time insisting on a real answer or an exact time when you can expect an answer.

When people say that they have to look into something and get back to you, about the only thing you can do (without making a rather obvious and frontal assault on their honesty) is wait. However, you *can* nail them down to a specific date and time that they will "get back to you." If the question is important enough for the other side to delay (or not answer at all), the issue is important enough for you to press forward. Asking, "When can I expect an answer from you?" is a direct way of obtaining that information. Be sure to make a note of the reply.

Don't accept an assertion for the answer

A person who doesn't want to answer your question may try instead to emphatically state something close to what you're looking for. This technique is common when you're asking for a commitment that the other party doesn't want to make.

Sometimes, an assertion about the past is substituted for an answer about the future. For example, you ask whether a company plans to spend $50,000 on advertising in the next year. You receive an emphatic statement that the company has spent $50,000 each year for the past four years, that sales are rising, and that any company would be a fool to cut back now. Don't settle for such assertions — push for an answer. Say something like "Does that mean that your company has made a final commitment to spend $50,000 for advertising this year?"

Because assertions are sometimes delivered with a great deal of energy or passion, you may feel awkward insisting on the answer to your question. Not persisting with the inquiry can be fatal to your interests.

Don't allow too many pronouns

Beware the deadly pronoun: he, she, they, especially the infamous *they* and the power-gilded *we*. Pronouns can send you into a quagmire of misunderstanding. During a negotiation, force your counterpart to use specific nouns and proper names. This preventive measure avoids a great deal of miscommunication.

With pronouns, you must guess which "they" or which "we" the speaker is talking about. Don't guess. Just throw up your hands and say, with humor, "Too many pronouns." I have never met anyone who begrudged me taking the time to clarify this issue. More often than not, the request is greeted with a chuckle. The potential for confusion is obvious, and everyone appreciates the effort to maintain clarity.

Look for Evidence of Listening

As you listen to the other party in a negotiation, be alert to the occasional indicators that the other person is not really listening to you. If the other person says something like "uh-huh" or "that's interesting," find out immediately whether this response is an expression of genuine interest, a way of postponing discussion, or — equally fatal to communication — a signal that he or she is fighting the dreaded doze monster. Those little demons that tug at the eyelids in the middle of the afternoon cause odd, nonspecific utterances to fall from the lips.

If you suspect the latter, ask a probing question or two to ferret out the truth. Asking, "'Uh-huh' yes you agree, or just 'Uh-huh' you heard me?" is a good way to flush out the non-committal uh-huh.

When someone says "That's interesting," find out exactly what makes it interesting. Don't be afraid to keep things lively. This approach is much better than having the conversation die right there at the negotiating table.

If you decide that, indeed, your conversational partner is simply not listening, take a break. Often, a quick stretch or, in a more serious case of the afternoon slumps, a walk around the block helps revive everybody. If a distraction is causing the lagging interest in what you are saying, deal with it. Discuss the preoccupying problem or have the distracted party make that critical call.

Chapter 4

Listening with All Your Senses

∙ ∙

In This Chapter

▶ Improving your listening skills on the path to success

▶ Listening to body language as well as verbal communications

∙ ∙

*L*istening is fundamental to every negotiation. Listen with your ears, your eyes, and every pore in between. Studies show that up to 65 percent of what we communicate is non-verbal. Listening and recognizing nonverbal cues are essential negotiation skills that give you a leg up in all kinds of situations. Not listening leads to failed deals, bad deals, and no deals.

At its simplest, *listening* is accurately taking in all the information that the other party is communicating. *Active listening* involves all the senses and many screening devices. At its most sophisticated, listening also involves getting the other party to open up, to communicate more information, and to express ideas more clearly than is the norm for that person.

Steps to Becoming a Good Listener

I have five ways you can improve your listening skills right now. The techniques I cover in the next sections are easy to use and bring immediate results.

In addition, try these two active listening tools in your very next conversation:

✔ **Restating:** Repeat, word-for-word, a short statement that the other person has just made to you. It's harder than you think. You won't use this technique all the time or in every circumstance, but it's a good way to start raising your own awareness level about listening.

✔ **Paraphrasing:** Recount, in your own words, the longer statements that the other person has said to you. You can use this technique far more often than restating. Don't be embarrassed if you get it wrong a lot when you first start paraphrasing back. This is a good technique to use when someone is making a dense presentation and you want to be sure that you understand it, every step of the way.

In either case, introduce your efforts with respect and good humor. Try starting with the phrase, "Let me see if I got that right. . . ."

A case of the "yeah, buts"

One of the most self-destructive ways to listen in business and personal situations is listening with what I call the "yeah, buts." This condition occurs when there is a kernel (or more) of truth in something negative that is being said but you don't want to hear it. You are defensive about what the speaker is saying, so the first response out of your mouth is "yeah, but." Whether you're listening to a customer, boss, or spouse, you've got to put the automatic "yeah, but" response on hold. Watch out for responses like these:

✔ "Yeah, I know, but you're not our only customer."

✔ "Yeah, but honey, you're always on my case about that."

✔ "Yeah, but *you* always use that tone of voice with me."

These responses keep you from hearing the other person. You block out any chance you have of learning something from this person. You want to say "I hear you" or "I understand" first. Then make sure that you do. Ask questions to find out as much as possible about what the other person is saying. Don't stop until you fully understand what is being said; then — and only then — you can try to explain the situation. You will get more positive results this way.

Clear away the clutter

Noise clutter, desk clutter, and even mind clutter all interfere with good listening. It also keeps others from listening to you.

- ✔ If you have something else on your mind, write it down before you enter a conversation. With a note as a reminder, you won't worry about forgetting to address the issue — and your mind is free to concentrate on the conversation.

- ✔ Clear your desk — or whatever is between you and the speaker — so you can focus on what the speaker is saying.

- ✔ Don't accept phone calls while you're talking with someone else. Interrupting a conversation to take a telephone call makes the person in the room with you feel unimportant and makes what you have to say seem unimportant.

- ✔ When you talk to someone, don't just mute the television or pull out one earbud, turn the distraction off.

When a co-worker comes to your office, don't feel that you need to engage in a discussion right away. If you know that you need to finish a task, try saying, "Just a minute, let me finish this so I can give you my full attention." If it's going to take a while, ask to schedule a meeting for later that day. The same rule holds true for phone conversations. Never try to negotiate on the telephone while you're reading a note from your assistant, catching up on filing, or doing research on the Internet. Your brain cannot simultaneously process the conflicting information from your eyes and from your ears. Both messages lose out.

Take notes

Regardless of whether you ever refer to your notes again, the mere act of writing down the salient points boosts the entire listening process. It's almost impossible to fully absorb an entire conversation of any length without making some written notes.

Making notes is important throughout every step of the negotiating process. Immediately after a negotiating session, review your notes to be sure that you wrote down everything you may want to recall, and that you can read everything you wrote down.

A confirming memo stating what you think you heard and verifying the material with the other side aids both parties. Even if your counterpart believes that you recorded the conversation incorrectly and rejects your version, you still win. Your memo serves an excellent purpose if the response reveals that you and your counterpart have conflicting views of the proceedings. Immediately thank the other party. Point out that you wrote the memo to be sure that you listened well and interpreted the discussion accurately.

People often change or refine their positions after they see them in black and white. Let that modification happen gracefully. When the other party provides a new version of the negotiation, don't argue about the past conversation. Fighting over who said what seldom furthers the negotiations; identifying the opposing party's position does.

Ask questions

Asking questions is so important that I devote all of Chapter 3 to various techniques of asking questions. Just remember that asking the right questions at the right times, and listening to the answers, can move a negotiation forward in a way that nothing else can.

Count to three

One extraordinarily simple device can help you listen more effectively: Count to three before you speak. This slight delay enables you to absorb and understand the last statement before you respond. The delay also announces that you have given some thought to what you are about to say.

Wake yourself up

If you are truly interested in what the other party is saying, look the part. Assuming an attentive position involves

- ✔ Keeping your eyes focused.
- ✔ Acknowledging the other party's words with a nod.
- ✔ Uncrossing your arms and legs.
- ✔ Sitting straight in the chair.
- ✔ Facing the speaker full on.
- ✔ Leaning forward.
- ✔ Making as much eye contact as you can.

If you feel yourself getting drowsy, sit up straighter or get your blood flowing in whatever way works for you.

Listening Your Way up the Corporate Ladder

In a negotiation, silence is golden — in fact, it's money in the bank. Many a negotiation has been blown — and many a sale lost — because someone kept talking long after discussion was necessary or desirable. Conversely, many an opportunity to gain valuable information has been lost because the listening activity stops too soon.

One of the best ways to control a meeting is to listen to everyone in the room. If a big talker is monopolizing the negotiation, instead of grabbing the floor yourself, point out someone else who looks as though he or she is trying to talk. "Jane, you look like you had a comment on that." Jane appreciates it, others appreciate it, and you suddenly control the meeting. If you find that you still have something to add, the group will probably let you do so. You are now a hero, even to members of the other negotiating team. When you do say something, everyone listens out of appreciation — if not admiration.

Various studies show that successful people listen better than their counterparts — especially on their way up. Some examples of the importance of listening effectively while you're on the clock:

- ✔ Many managers face setbacks in their careers when they prejudge an employee before they hear all sides of the story. If you want to gain respect as a manager, gather all the data from all the parties before you take any action.

✔ New employees need to listen first when they enter a meeting or a department. Get the lay of the land. Resist that first verbal contribution, which will be everyone's first impression of you, until you know that the contribution is a good one.

✔ Salespeople lose sales when they talk more than they listen. The successful ones use empathetic statements to show they understand what the customer is saying and how he or she is feeling.

Listening to Body Language

Verbal and written communications are not the only elements of communication in a negotiation — or in life. Good negotiators only get better when they draw meaning and insight from the way a person stands or sits, the way a person dresses, or the panoply of facial expressions that play out during a conversation. *Body language* refers to all the ways people communicate *without* speaking or writing.

Honing your ability to use and understand body language is one of the most enjoyable ways to improve negotiating skills. If you're not already fluent in body language, practice it. The knowledge will allow you to become a smarter negotiator by recognizing such things as resistance, boredom, and nervousness, all of which can hamper a negotiation.

Matching your body language with your words

Make sure that *your* body language expresses the message you want to send and that your body language matches your words, if you want your words to be believed. If you are enthusiastic about a project, show that enthusiasm in your body. Don't recline relaxed on the sofa. The message of disinterest communicated by your body will be remembered far longer than the words of interest that come out of your mouth.

Several reasons may explain why your body language may not match your words.

✔ **You're having an energy drain.** When you're tired, keeping your body properly expressive takes extra energy. Feed the left side of your brain with positive thoughts. Stand up or walk around to get your blood flowing. If you have to, step outside for a moment to reignite your energy.

✔ **You're not concentrating on the communication of the moment.** Many gestures, movements, and mannerisms indicate that a person is actually thinking about a matter other than the current topic of conversation. If you find your mind wandering, the other side will quickly see it in your face. Ask for a break so you can make a phone call and clear a concern out of your mind. Your physical presence may be much less important than your mental presence.

✔ **You have developed bad communication habits.** A classic comic sketch illustrates this point: The disgusted spouse utters a terse, "Fine" with lips clamped tight, letting his partner know that things are anything but fine. The body language trumps the spoken word.

A listener gets the nonverbal message much more clearly than the verbal message.

Reading someone else's body language

Being able to accurately read the true attitude and feelings of someone across the table can be enormously important. Based on what you learn about the other person's mood or attitude, you can temper your own words and actions appropriately — for example, you can calm down someone who's agitated or perk up someone who's bored.

Discover how much fun you can have reading the body language of others. The more you practice this skill, the better you will be at negotiating. Try reading body language in different situations:

✔ **At an event connected to your work:** Pause a moment at the door. Instead of looking for someone you know, look over the room. Identify the more influential people. Try to distinguish who wields power. Who are the employers? Who are the employees? What differences in body language make social status apparent?

✔ **At a social gathering:** See if you can spot very outgoing people. Who is shy? Are any of the couples fighting?

✔ **At an airport or shopping mall:** Watch people talk on their cell phones and guess who's on the other end of the line just by observing body language. If a person is cradling the phone, with head cocked and body draped languidly, a romantic interest is probably on the other end. If the person is shifting from foot to foot and looking around, an uncomfortable personal call is probably taking place. If the caller is standing erect and staring down at some notes or looking straight ahead in concentration, the call is most likely business related.

Interpreting conflicting messages

Reading the body language of another person is not a trick to gain advantage, it's a tool to improve communication. People who are exhibiting incongruous body language are frequently unaware of the fact that their spoken words and their true feelings are not consistent. By drawing out those differences and reconciling them, you do a great service for your side and for the person with whom you are negotiating.

If you pick up an incongruity between what a person's body is saying and what that person's mouth is saying, you can assume that something is going on. You want to take a reality check and start asking the person questions about what he or she is thinking and feeling. It's usually one of the following:

✔ The person is unaware of his or her effect on others.

✔ The person's body language is expressing a hidden agenda.

✔ The person is tired or is confused.

The next sections talk about common body-language incongruities.

The nervous laugh

One of the most common examples of body language not matching the situation is the *nervous laugh*. A laugh that isn't a reaction to anything humorous signals nervousness or discomfort.

If you hear a nervous laugh, let a few beats go by and then turn directly to the source of the laughter and encourage that person to verbalize his or her feelings by asking a related question. If pricing has been under discussion, you may say: "Julius, how do you feel about the pricing structure?" Often, the person won't admit to having any concerns, but keep probing. You may have to return to the subject a few times, rephrasing your request until the truth comes out.

Positive words but negative body language

Many employees complain that their supervisors give mixed messages with body language. The words are positive, but the body language is negative. For example, your boss calls you in for a meeting. She says, "Good morning," and begins to discuss your recent improvement in punctuality. However, her arms are crossed at the waist, and her head is angled away from you so that she's looking at you sideways. You know that these are negative signals (see Table 4-1). If you have the guts, you may venture, "It looks to me like something may be bothering you." Your boss may be forthright about her annoyance, or she may deny her true feelings with a sharp reply, "What makes you think anything is bothering me?"

Blind spots

If you get conflicting verbal and nonverbal messages from someone, but that person denies that a discrepancy exists, you are witnessing a *blind spot* — something you know about others that they themselves are not conscious of. Blind spots cause miscommunications and resentment.

In a negotiation, if you suspect the other party has a blind spot, you need to take frequent reality checks. Check out your understanding with your counterpart's body language. You may even begin with the statement, "I need a reality check." Then go right into your reading: "I sense I have lost you," or "I sense we should take a break." If you take responsibility for your need, your counterpart is less likely to be defensive, and you are more likely to get truthful information. This way you may get at your opponent's true feelings. Sometimes you even uncover some underlying interests.

Most people have at least one blind spot — one area in which they don't really know how their words or actions are affecting people. Blind spots are like bad breath — everyone knows except the person who has it. The best way to find your own blind spot is to invite feedback.

If the blind spot belongs to another, you need to ask the person if he or she wants your feedback. If the response is no, believe it. You may need to find a higher-up to deal with the issue — someone the individual *must* listen to.

Emphasizing with body language

Pound the table. Wave your arms. Jump up and down. These are a few of the classic ways you can use your body language for emphasis. However, save these demonstrations until you need them. If you use loudness throughout a negotiation, the added volume carries no special meaning when you really need it.

The key to emphasis is a change from the norm. Body language always involves a cluster of movements. It should naturally be tied into voice levels, tempo, and loudness. Sometimes, you can create extra emphasis by exhibiting body language that runs counter to the communication. For example, you may lean forward and quietly, slowly say that you are very, very angry. Here the emphasis is created just as powerfully — maybe more so — than if you yelled at the top of your lungs.

Surprises can occur in any negotiation. Generally speaking, however, you should know going into a negotiating session what will and won't be important. Hold back your emphasis until you get to the stuff that is really important to you. This strategy is why a good negotiator lets the merely annoying issues slide by and saves the emphasis for the truly important points.

How to Use Body Language in Your Negotiations

From the moment you walk into a negotiation, observe the body language of everybody in the room. During the negotiation, keep observing your opponent's body language. Focus on the four channels: face and head, arms and hands, legs and feet, and torso. When you are so focused on the total person who is talking to you, you will listen better. Your observations of body language will help you pick up unstated nuances such as what items are more important, and what items are less important to the other side.

Complete shifts in body language during a negotiation can be more telling than isolated signals. These shifts reveal that an issue is vitally important or is causing stress to the other party. Any shifts from your counterpart's normal position may very well indicate that the person you're dealing with has changed in attitude in some way. Being aware of this body language can be particularly important if the other party

✔ Feels that you are talking about a sensitive issue

✔ Is losing interest

✔ Needs a break or a stretch

✔ Is turning off to your arguments

The shifts in body language can be yellow caution lights telling you to proceed slowly, look, and listen. In the extreme, they are red lights telling you to stop now! Don't go further without taking a break. They can also be green lights telling you to go in for the close.

Don't ignore nonverbal signals. You may even want to include your observations in your written notes just as you include spoken words. This record helps build familiarity with the other person's unspoken vocabulary. Everybody uses body language differently.

Knowing where to stand

One of the most important observations you can make about a room full of people is the personal space each person commands. During conversation, for example, people don't lean closely into the space of an important person they think has greater standing than they do (either in wealth, influence, power, or social status).

Spatial relationships come into play when you set up a room for a meeting. Almost intuitively, people know that an important negotiation warrants a table large enough to keep a formal distance between people. If someone must dominate a meeting, that person is seated at the head of the table.

Seating in a meeting is important, because once the spatial relationships are established, they are not easy to change.

Making the first contact

One of the best ways you can begin a meeting is with great body language. Let your enthusiasm and energy show. Stick out your hand. Meet the other person's eyes and give a good, firm handshake.

If you don't own a good handshake, develop one now. Let the flesh between your thumb and forefinger meet the other person's flesh between the thumb and forefinger. Press — do not squeeze — the hand. One pump accompanied by eye contact is plenty. One or two more may express great enthusiasm; any more than that can make the person uncomfortable.

The landscape for making the first contact has broadened. For instance, women greeting women in America can touch both hands at the same time as an alternative to a handshake. A hug, even in a business meeting, is appropriate if the relationship between two people warrants this familiarity. Increasingly, hugs between men and women, or two men or two women who know each other, are common. A classic male show of power is to shake hands in the normal fashion and reach with the left hand to also grip the man's elbow.

However, as you begin taking more careful note of body language and how people relate to each other, you will notice that the space between two people still reveals a lot about the relationship. Friends may stand a foot apart, but you would not stand that close to someone you were being introduced to for the very first time.

Showing that you're receptive (and knowing if your counterpart isn't)

If you pay attention to body language early in a negotiation, you can spot signals of how *receptive* (that is, how ready to listen and how open to your ideas) your counterpart is. Consider eye contact, for example. Research shows that, during conversation, people look at each other between 30 and 60 percent of the time. A listener who meets your eyes less than 30 percent of the time is probably unreceptive.

Table 4-1 shows some positive and negative cues associated with being receptive and unreceptive. You probably don't ever want to look unreceptive, but you do want to notice if others are unreceptive, so you become familiar with the negative cues as well as the positive ones.

Table 4-1	Body Language of Receptive and Unreceptive Listeners	
Body Channel	*Receptive (Positive Cues)*	*Unreceptive (Negative Cues)*
Facial expressions and eyes	Smiles, much eye contact, more interest in the person than in what is being said	No eye contact or squinted eyes, jaw muscles clenched, cheeks twitching with tension, head turned slightly away from the speaker so the eye contact is a sidelong glance
Arms and hands	Arms spread, hands open on the table, relaxed in the lap, or on the arms of a chair	Hands clenched, arms crossed in front of the chest, hand over the mouth or rubbing the back of the neck
Legs and feet	Sitting: Legs together, or one in front of the other slightly (as if at the starting line of a race). Standing: Weight evenly distributed, hands on hips, body tilted toward the speaker	Standing: Crossed legs, pointing away from the speaker. Sitting or standing: Legs and feet pointing toward the exit.
Torso	Sitting on the edge of the chair, unbuttoning suit coat, body tilted toward the speaker	Leaning back in the chair stiffly, suit coat remains buttoned

Receptive people look relaxed with open hands, displaying the palms, indicating an openness to discussion. The more of the palm that is visible, the greater the receptivity of the person. They lean forward, whether they are sitting or standing. Receptive male negotiators unbutton their coats.

By contrast, people who aren't willing to listen may keep their hands on their hips, lean back in the chair, or protectively fold their arms across their chest. People who aren't receptive clench their hands into a fist or tightly grip some other body part. Having one leg up on the arm of the chair often appears to be an open posture, but watch out, this position may signal a lack of consideration, especially if the office doesn't belong to the person demonstrating this behavior. Figure 4-1 shows the typical body language of someone who's receptive and someone who definitely is not.

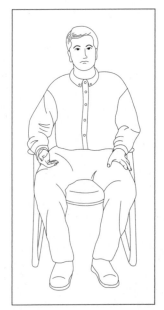 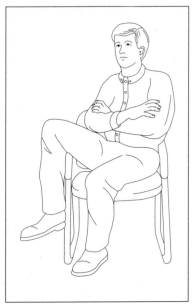

Figure 4-1: Which individual would you rather negotiate with?

Studies show that parties are more likely to reach an agreement if they begin a negotiation displaying receptive body language (shown on the left in Figure 4-1). This result appears to be true whether the stance was an unconscious decision or a contrived strategy for beginning a meeting in a positive manner. In addition, the defensive postures are also contagious. If one person assumes a defensive posture and holds that position for any period of time, you can actually watch others in the room adopting the same position.

Seeing a change of heart

Observing how someone is sitting or standing (refer to Table 4-1 or Figure 4-1) is only the first step in reading body language. Positions and gestures change with attitudes and emotions. These shifts may mean that the person is getting restless, or they may mean a shift up or down in the person's acceptance level.

As someone's acceptance of your ideas grows, you may notice the following indicators:

- Cocking the head
- Squinting the eyes slightly
- Uncrossing the legs
- Leaning forward
- Scooting to the edge of the chair
- Increasing eye contact
- Touching the forehead or chin, as in the statue *The Thinker*
- Touching you (if the movement is to reassure, and not to interrupt)

Just as you can gauge increasing acceptance to your ideas by watching body language, you can also notice signs of increasing resistance to your ideas. For example, if someone clutches the back of his neck with his palm, you can interpret this gesture quite literally as, "This message is a pain in the neck." Other gestures of resistance:

- Fidgeting nervously (cannot accept what is being said)
- Reducing eye contact (cannot accept what is being said)

- ✔ Placing hands behind one's back (indicates an attempt to stay in control of oneself — resisting the urge to act out verbally or physically)

- ✔ Placing a hand over one's mouth (may indicate an attempt to hold back a negative comment)

- ✔ Locking ankles

- ✔ Gripping one's arm or wrist

- ✔ Crossing the arms in front of the chest

- ✔ Squinting one's eyes dramatically

- ✔ Making fistlike gestures

- ✔ Twisting the feet or the entire body so they point to the door

Ferreting out boredom

One of the most important body language messages to look for during any conversation, but especially in a negotiation, is an indication of boredom. Looking out the window, holding the head up with one hand, doodling in a way that seems to absorb the doodler's complete attention, drumming fingers on the table — all these indicate that the listener is no longer paying attention. People who are losing interest may be shifting in their seats, fidgeting, or pointing their feet toward the exit.

Negotiating charades

You can modify the familiar game of charades to sensitize yourself to the importance and meaning of body language. These two formats seem to work best:

- ✔ Someone can mime an emotion, and the other players must identify it. This game is simple and fun, and it demonstrates

the variety of nonverbal communications available in face-to face communications.

- ✔ Players can mime an entire negotiation — either individually or as teams. The other team or player is required to figure out specifically what the negotiation is about and what positions are represented.

What should you do if you notice that the other party in your negotiation is showing signs of boredom? Don't start speaking louder or faster, as you may be tempted to do. Instead, say, "Wait. I need a reality check. I'm sensing that I'm losing you. What's happening?" And then listen. You may find out what's really keeping this person or group from accepting your idea. Doing a reality check can save a great deal of time and win you respect as a person who is perceptive and willing to risk hearing the truth. This fact alone makes huge points in your favor during any negotiation.

Wearing your confidence on your sleeve

During a negotiation, projecting confidence is important. A lack of self-confidence can result in nervousness. If your body language reveals that you are nervous, your counterpart may deem that you're not secure enough to maintain a strong position in the negotiation and may be less inclined to compromise on the terms in an effort to reach an agreement.

In addition to making sure that your body language expresses self-assurance, you can also benefit from being able to gauge your counterpart's confidence level. This awareness of the other party's strength as a negotiator can help you determine your own goals, limits, opening offers, and attempts to close the deal. Watching body language is the key to assessing your counterpart's degree of comfort during the negotiation.

Just like children, adults who get nervous tend to fidget in their chairs (although this behavior can also indicate boredom or preoccupation with other matters). Nervous fidgeting can also include putting hands into the mouth, tugging at clothing, jingling change, fiddling with items in a purse, or fondling any personal object. When people are nervous, they often increase their distance from those they are negotiating with. Nervous people frequently verbalize their condition without using words through throat clearing, oral pauses, or guttural sounds.

Confident people may place their hands in a steeple position (touching the fingertips of both hands together to form what looks like a church steeple). Sitting up straight and using frequent eye contact also shows confidence. Someone who is confident physically sits on a level slightly higher than anybody else. Propping your feet up is not just an expression of confidence, but an act of claiming territory. If you can put your feet on something, you own it.

Closing the deal

Closing a negotiation often means *closing in*. Intimate distance — touching or being 6 to 18 inches apart — is usually reserved for personal, affectionate interactions. However, you may find yourself or your counterpart naturally moving that close as you reach more agreements and draw nearer to closing the deal. A good salesperson knows that an appropriate touch on the customer's forearm or hand cements the deal.

The body language of acceptance varies widely from one individual to another. The exact point in time at which you get concurrence is more often marked with slight nuances than raucous outbursts. Seldom does someone jump up in joy at the moment of making the decision to close a deal. In my experience, the bigger the deal, the more subtle the display at that magic moment when the other side makes the mental commitment to close the deal. The terms are then generally reviewed by both sides to be sure that the deal is acceptable.

If you close a deal, don't forget to carry out the terms of the agreement. This follow-up is important. There is no bigger let-down than to shake hands on a deal and then not hear from the other side for days. Be sure to take the next step. If it isn't your direct responsibility, keep checking with the person who is responsible. You are the person who closed the deal, so your integrity is on the line.

Don't Believe Everything You See

Body language augments rather than replaces the spoken word. The meanings of certain actions or gestures can vary depending on the circumstances and the individual. Consider these examples:

✔ Sitting erect may indicate a stiff bargaining position, or it may indicate a stiff back. Stay alert to the body language, but combine your observations with the spoken words to determine the correct meaning.

✔ Gestures of anger are used when a person is genuinely angry; however, these actions can also be employed for effect. Some people are just blustery by nature.

Evaluate body language cautiously, just as you do all the other information that comes to you during a negotiation.

Different strokes for different folks

No matter how much you know about body language in general, don't grow overconfident when applying your knowledge to a specific person — especially someone you don't know very well. Each individual has unique body language.

Consider the context

As you become more sensitive to body language, you become more conscious of the differences in the meanings of gestures. A clenched fist usually represents anger. Held firmly above the head, it can be a symbol of quiet rage. Pumped up and down, especially if the person is also jumping and squealing, a clenched fist can be an expression of extreme joy.

Prepare for the bluff

Most adults have the art of "faking it" pretty well perfected. People are prone to hide their real feelings in a business setting. Negotiators may display all the signs of accepting a deal, although their true reaction is quite the opposite. When you think the other side is accepting your proposal, try to close the deal. That provides a good check on your reading of the other party's body language. If you can't close, what you observed was something other than acceptance. Don't be fooled the next time you see the same reaction from that person — and keep trying to close.

Smiles are almost always an expression of happiness. However, society sometimes requires a smile when the soul is not happy. The mouth drawn tightly and obligingly back reveals a devotion to duty more than merriment. And a half-smile (one corner of the mouth crooked upward) reveals a wry feeling of superiority — like the smile on the face of the bad guy just before he shoots the good guy in an old Western.

Most of the differences between the body language you see and the intended spirit of the communication are accidental. These differences are generally not the result of a sinister plot. The impact on you will be the same if you are misled. This chapter helps keep you from being misled by body language that is different from the message of the spoken word. When you make such an observation, don't assume that the other person is intentionally trying to mislead you.

You can read more about body language with the two seminal works: *Body Language,* by Julius Fast, and *How to Read a Person Like a Book,* by Gerard I. Nierenberg and Henry H. Calero. Both books contain very good bibliographies. A more recent book worth reading is *Reading People: How to Understand People and Predict Their Behavior — Anytime, Anyplace* by Jo-Ellan Dimitrius and Mark Mazzarella. Dimitrius, a renowned jury consultant, provides a wealth of tips for ferreting out people's viewpoints, motives, and character traits. And, by all means, look into the granddaddy of them all: *The Expression of the Emotions in Man and Animals,* written by Charles Darwin and first published in 1872.

Chapter 5

Being Crystal Clear: Telling It Like It Is

● ●

In This Chapter

▶ Organizing your thoughts

▶ Being clear during a negotiation

▶ Capturing an audience

▶ Avoiding the pitfalls of not being clear

● ●

Raw power flows from the simple ability to be clear and accurate in every step of a negotiation. Unfortunately, no one is born knowing how to express ideas clearly. This chapter is actually a short course in communication skills, showing you how to speak, write, and conduct yourself clearly at every stage of a negotiation.

The ability to communicate clearly is one of the six basic negotiating skills, which I list in Chapter 1. With practice, you can see how communication skills impact a negotiation and tell when your negotiation is faltering because of weak communication.

What Being Clear Means

In many ways, clear communication is the other side of effective listening (see Chapter 4). Just as you cannot listen *too* well, there is no such thing as being *too* clear. You can be too blunt, too fast, and too slow. You can't be too clear.

Being clear simply means that when you speak, write, or otherwise communicate, your listener understands your intended message. Sounds simple enough. Why aren't more people successful at it?

The reason more people are not good communicators is that they communicate from this point of view: What do *I* want to tell my listener? How am *I* going to appear? What are they going to think of *me?* Not effective. Your point of view must be from the listener's side of the communication. Ask yourself these questions: What does my listener need to know? What information does my listener need to make a decision? What is my listener's knowledge of the subject?

First, you must be clear with yourself about what information you're trying to get across. Then you must know who the listener is, what filters are in place, and how to get through those filters so you can be understood.

Organizing Your Thoughts for Clarity

Before you can organize your thoughts, you need to assess what your listener needs and then find out how experienced he or she is with the subject matter. When you know that, you can figure out how much of your presentation needs to focus on general education — bringing the other person up to speed.

You can organize your thoughts in many ways, but the important thing is to do it. The next sections present my favorite three ways to organize a presentation.

P.R.E.P. for a presentation

The key words for the P.R.E.P technique are *point, reason, example, point.* For example:

- ✔ **My point is:** Exercise is energizing.
- ✔ **The reason is:** It gets your heart rate up.

> ✔ **My example is:** After at least 20 to 30 minutes of increased heart rate, you are more energized when you come out of the gym than when you went in.
>
> ✔ **So, my point is:** Exercise is energizing.

The P.R.E.P. approach works because it's so logical. This formula works with any presentation, from a five-minute informal chat, to a thirty-minute formal speech using many examples. The P.R.E.P. approach is a great way to get organized and be clear.

Outline your points

Another strategy is to list and number your points. The following is an example:

> I recommend that you hire the consultant to create a plan that will
>
> 1. Increase sales
>
> 2. Improve morale
>
> 3. Generate productivity

Tell 'em once, tell 'em twice, tell 'em again

Here's the classic standby used by presenters and writers across the country:

> ✔ Tell 'em what you're gonna tell 'em.
>
> ✔ Tell 'em.
>
> ✔ Tell 'em what you told 'em.

I use this one a lot because it drives a point home.

Being Clear

A well-turned phrase always involves an element of art. Part of the beauty of a clear phrase is how accurately it hits the bull's-eye; that is, how precisely it conveys your meaning. For best results, take your time. If something is worth saying, it's worth saying clearly.

Asking, "Did I make myself clear?" often helps both parties proceed more productively. A question may remind the other person to listen instead of lazily replying "yes." If the point is critical, you may ask the other party to repeat the information back to you just to be sure that you're communicating effectively. Assure your counterpart that repeating vital information does not constitute an agreement — just clarification.

Know your purpose or goals

When you know exactly what you want to say, communicating clearly is much easier. In the past, you must have had the urge to say, "So, what's your point?" — usually with an exasperated tone. More often than not, a person who is asked that question looks surprised and fumbles for a good, one-sentence answer. When the speaker doesn't know the point, the listener is hopelessly lost.

In any communication, you should know the point and be keenly aware of the overall purpose or goal. When you're trying to get someone else to provide some action, approval, or acquiescence (that is, if you are in a negotiation), you need to have your short- and long-range goals in mind.

Cut the mumbo-jumbo

Some concepts are, by nature, just plain difficult to grasp. Sometimes being clear requires creativity. For example, if you have many numbers to present, try putting them in graphs — bar, pie, or line charts — anything but reams of numbers. Keep the lists of numbers as a backup.

By all means, oversimplify technical points at first — you can explain fully later in the conversation, after you have your listeners hooked. Also, define jargon and spell out acronyms. Avoid references that may leave your listener wondering what the heck you're taking about. In written materials, footnotes and appendices serve the purpose of clarity. Do everything you can to make listening and understanding easy and enjoyable.

Keep your commitments

Being clear includes being consistent in the words you say and the deeds that follow. If you say one thing and do another, it's confusing. Your inconsistent conduct turns an otherwise clear communication into a real puzzlement. Keep each and every commitment that you make during a negotiation. In life, keeping commitments is important; in a negotiation, it's essential.

If you tell the other party that you will call back at 9 the next morning, be sure to call at that time. Breaking your promise calls your integrity into question and creates confusion about what exactly you meant when you promised to call back at 9 a.m. Failing to keep your word also upsets the other party. Such inattention may be considered, debated, and evaluated by the other side. Their loss of trust may call into question side issues and create tensions that are counterproductive to a negotiation.

Write it down

The written word is often more useful than the spoken word when you're trying to communicate clearly. When you have something to say, write it down, look at it, edit it, and make it right. When the words are your own, you don't have to release them until they are as near to perfect as possible.

Many people believe they can't or don't know how to write as clearly as they speak. This is rarely true. The simple fact is that when you write instead of speak the words, you can see more easily whether your message is unclear. You can see in black and white that the words are ambiguous or your thoughts are incomplete.

These basic tips get you on the road to clear communication:

✔ Use short sentences.

✔ Use short words.

✔ Avoid jargon and abbreviations — even when you are writing to another professional in your field — unless the other person uses these terms exactly the way that you do.

✔ Complete your sentences.

✔ Stick to one idea per paragraph.

✔ Have a beginning, middle, and end to the overall communication.

✔ Be accurate.

 Don't be afraid to number paragraphs to cover different points, but don't delude yourself into thinking that numbering paragraphs brings order to a document that otherwise lacks coherence or good sense.

Try being a journalist

When you think of clear writing, the most common reference point is your daily newspaper. Every school of journalism in the country teaches students about the "five horsemen" of journalism: Who?, What?, Where?, When?, and Why? The journalist is supposed to answer these five questions in the first paragraph of a story. The next five paragraphs should each expand on the answer to one of the questions. The least important information appears at the end of the story. That way, if the story is too long for the available space in the newspaper, editors can just delete the end of story, and no important information is lost.

Use the same technique, and you can't go wrong. Remember: You're providing the information your listener needs to know to achieve *your* goal. Organize the facts like a newspaper story.

Steering Others to Clarity

Nobody wants to be a bad communicator, but sometimes people need a bit of help to be clear. When the other party is not being clear, your job is to steer that person toward concise communication. Don't just toss them this book (although it may make a nice gift). Coax from your counterpart a clear statement of intentions, wants, and needs. Your technique for acquiring this information depends on the type of person you are dealing with. The following sections contain some tips for accomplishing this important task. Each section is devoted to a personality type you may encounter.

Tangent people

Some people are not clear because they go off on a tangent, and then another tangent, and another. To deal with them:

- ✔ Listen up to a point. You are listening especially for a good point to break into their discourse so you can bring them back to the topic.

- ✔ Be assertive when you interrupt. Not impolite, but firm.

- ✔ Your first statement should be a validation, "Yes, you're right. Now, as to the purpose . . ." That's how you get people with this type of communication pattern back on track.

Interrupters

These people even interrupt themselves. They lose their train of thought while they are speaking and tend to jump from point to point. Your best practices include

- ✔ Taking careful notes. Write a topic heading. Make notes, and when the speaker switches topics, leave a lot of space before you write a new topic heading. When the speaker switches back to a previous topic, go back to that topic section and continue your note taking.

- ✔ Concentrating and staying focused. This is hard work.

- ✔ Reminding the speaker of the most recent statement before the interruption. Don't leave until you get a specific answer.

- ✔ Being appropriate as you present your own specific questions.

Unprepared people

Some people may have difficulty getting fully prepared for negotiations. You can do one of two things:

- ✔ Postpone the meeting.

- ✔ Conduct the meeting at the unprepared party's office. Tactfully invite your counterpart's support people who may know more about the subject.

Too busy to be clear

These important people don't think they can take the time to be clear. When encountering busy people:

- ✔ Schedule meetings at the beginning of the day to avoid distractions and ensure everyone's full attention.

- ✔ Guard against interruptions; for example, request the person hold his or her calls for ten minutes in order to get information.

- ✔ Be efficient in meetings — have a written agenda even for a two-person meeting. The agenda shows the other person how much you value his or her time.

- ✔ Show you are taking notes and recording comments.

- ✔ Be appropriate but keep pressing for the details you need.

Sometimes, you need to steer your boss to clarity. The next time the boss slams papers on your desk and says, "We need this yesterday," do the following:

1. **Stifle the urge to answer "in your dreams."**

2. **Respond with a positive, "Yes, absolutely — will do."**

   After all, this *is* the boss. And this reply will relax your employer because it's what any boss wants to hear.

3. **Ask for prioritization.**

   This step is essential: Because you are already *fully aware* of your priorities and the allotted time to accomplish them, answer, "Here's the situation, Boss. I've got these other two priorities you want by 3 o'clock today. Which of these can be put off until tomorrow?"

By following these steps, you force the boss to be clear. Your boss needs to prioritize — that's a boss's job. Sometimes your boss will go away without making any further demands, realizing that you are already working on important projects.

Capturing an Audience

Clarity makes you a good presenter during a negotiation. These tips can help you get through your next negotiation when the spotlight is on you:

✔ **Analyze your audience.** Put yourself in your counterparts' shoes. Try to anticipate what outcome they seek from the negotiation. After you gauge what your audience wants, you can figure out how best to sell your ideas of the negotiation at hand.

✔ **Set your goal and keep it handy.** Decide what outcome you would like to achieve as a result of the negotiation. Make sure that everything you say and do contributes to that outcome. Make sure that you stress your key points. If you are making a formal presentation at the beginning of a negotiation on a large project, consider giving your audience an outline of your presentation so they can follow along. It also gives you a measure of control on what information they take away.

✔ **Do your homework.** Research. Research. Research. Anticipate questions, and make sure you have the facts to back them up. Always prepare so you're ready for any emergency such as a well-aimed question from one of your counterparts. Practice until you know you are prepared to tackle any question thrown at you. Remember, your time in front of a group is your showcase.

✔ **Confidence is the key.** You have to be confident to show confidence. Have faith in yourself and your abilities. Think about how your presentation will help your audience to get what they want. Your goal remains fixed. Your job is to convince your listeners that your goal is something they want for their side also.

✔ **Plan your presentation.** Make a list of all the points you plan to discuss. Group your topics of discussion into sections and put the sections in the order that best achieves your objectives keeping in mind why your audience would want to hear what you have to say.

✔ **Plan your format and delivery.** Speak loud and clear. Don't mumble. Don't put your hand near your mouth, obscuring the sound of your voice. If needed, use your outline to guide you through your discussion. Don't make your presentation monotonous.

The most exciting idea in the world will fall on deaf ears if it's presented in a boring manner. Conversely, audiences have been known to rally around some pretty lame ideas when they were fired up by a persuasive speaker.

> ✔ **Manage expectations.** Communication is a two-way street. Before you begin your negotiation, be sure everyone in the room knows what to expect. Your advance communication about your presentation needs to be clear to set the perceptions right so no one is confused or disappointed.

Barriers to Clarity

The biggest barriers to clarity are your own fears and lack of concentration. You fear that if you make yourself clearly understood, an adverse reaction will follow — some vague, unspoken, definitely unwanted reaction. Identify those fears and work to make them less of a roadblock.

Fear of rejection

Everyone has a built-in fear of rejection. The natural inclination is to avoid rejection by blurring lines, being unclear, and failing to state your case accurately. But doing so just leaves you open to the rejection you fear along with frustrated cries of "Why didn't you say so in the first place?"

If an accurate statement of intent would cause the deal to fall apart, being clear is even more important. When you close a deal without being clear, the parties have different understandings and expectations. You are finalizing a bad deal. In fact, you are closing a deal that cannot possibly work.

Fear of hurting someone else

Often, people avoid hurting the feelings of others not out of compassion, but out of self-protection. Everyone wants to be liked; no one wants to be shunned.

Being clear and being confrontational are two different things. If you have bad news to deliver, do so with dignity and respect for the person's feelings. Even if you feel, in every fiber of your being, that the person is overreacting to your news, don't say so. Let the feelings run their course. But don't flinch or amend your statement. Just wait. This, too, shall pass. Being clear in such situations takes strength and confidence. Never sacrifice clarity to avoid confrontation.

General distractions

Other barriers to clarity can be

- **Fatigue:** You may be just plain tired and unable to focus. Sometimes a brisk walk outdoors revives you. Good nutrition and adequate rest are requirements for a master negotiator. But, in a pinch, an occasional dose of caffeine works, too.

- **Laziness:** You may not have prepared well enough and you are dreading being clear on some facts that are unsubstantiated. If this situation strikes a familiar chord, do your homework.

- **Interruptions:** Your listener may be doodling or not making eye contact. The room temperature may be extreme. Noise levels may be too high for you to be heard clearly. Hopefully, you are assertive enough to request these changes appropriately.

If the conversation or negotiation is important, be sure that you are well rested, prepared, and in an environment where clear communications can be heard.

The High Cost of Not Being Clear

I realize that my clarion call for clarity flies in the face of advice you may receive from people who say that ambiguity is the lubricant of negotiations. This nonprofessional attitude not only prolongs a bad myth about negotiating, it has spilled blood, cost lives, and wasted millions of dollars, drachmas, and dreams.

Deals that disappear

A common example of lack of clarity occurs when one party intentionally makes an unrealistic opening offer. If an outrageous trial balloon doesn't get the expected reaction (shock, disbelief, laughter, and ultimately bursting of the balloon), the person who made the offer often recounts, with great animation, that the other person "didn't even bat an eye."

It would be difficult to ascertain what percentage of negotiations never get underway because the initial demand was too high. I believe that it happens more often than most people suspect. The person who is turned off may never say a word to the party making the demand. Think of your own behavior. If you think the prices in a boutique are outrageous, do you say so? Or do you smile at the shopkeeper and say, "Just looking"? So when communicating opening offers, make sure you are clear about what you want — don't let a deal go sour because you weren't clear about your actual intentions.

The prices you pay without even knowing

Deals that don't close are to be expected if you're not clear during the negotiations. The harder item to assess is how the dynamic of the discussion changes when communications are not clear.

When you aren't clear, the other party feels insecure. Rather than confront you on your lack of clarity, the person you're negotiating with often compensates in one of two ways:

- ✔ **Reciprocal obfuscation:** That term simply means that the other party starts to be unclear, too. (I love the irony of using a hard-to-understand phrase to describe things that are hard to understand.) The other party doesn't know where you stand, so they don't feel comfortable making a clear commitment either. This situation substantially slows down a negotiation and may make productive communication almost impossible.

- ✔ **Leaving lots of room to maneuver:** If you are not clear, others won't feel safe enough to tell you specifically what they want. Rather than commit to a position, your counterpart will leave lots of room to maneuver, until you clarify where you want to end up.

These consequences are almost impossible to detect. Instead, you begin blaming the lack of clarity or indecisiveness on the other party. If you run into one of these behaviors, see whether the problem didn't start with you. Even if it didn't — even if you are dealing with someone who is naturally unclear or reluctant to take a position — you can push that person to greater clarity or decisiveness by communicating more clearly yourself.

Worst case: The deal closes

When a lack of clarity is a major factor in a negotiation, the biggest disasters occur when the deal closes and no one realizes that confusion remains. When written contracts are to follow, a lack of clarity is usually caught by the lawyers during the drafting stage, and the ambiguity can be worked out.

In a less formal situation, the confusion generally isn't discovered until much later. When that happens, both sides feel cheated and misled. People are rarely neutral about the cause of miscommunications. Blame is never far behind the discovery that the two parties failed to communicate well. The acrimony often permanently damages the relationship between the parties. The fallout often damages reputations, too.

The truth of the matter is that the results of an intentional lie and a mere miscommunication are often about the same. Preventing an innocent miscommunication is well worth the extra energy expended.

Phrases You Should Never Use during a Negotiation

Certain phrases go "clunk" against the ear every time you hear them. The following list covers some phrases that have little place in life, let alone a negotiation. If you hear one or more of these utterances come out of your mouth, stop immediately. Laugh about the slip or apologize, but don't assume that yellow caution lights didn't pop up for your listener when you uttered one of these trite, clumsy phrases:

> ✔ **"Trust me":** When someone says "trust me" as a substitute for providing the specific details you requested, be very cautious. Ask again for a commitment. Explain that it's not a question of trust, but an acknowledgment of the fact that circumstances change and that the agreement

must be enforceable, even if the current negotiators are no longer accessible. You want an agreement so clear that you don't have to trust the other person.

✔ **"I'm going to be honest with you":** Those who are always reassuring you about their honesty probably aren't being very honest with you.

✔ **"Take it or leave it":** Presenting a deal as a "take it or leave it" proposition is a mistake. It hurts you in the long run because you look like a bully. Even if the other side accepts what may be a reasonable offer, the deal leaves them feeling bad about the decision.

If you're are feeling frustrated and anticipating a refusal, push the pause button (see Chapter 6).

If you hear this phrase, don't let a bad negotiating style confuse you. Figure out if the offer is acceptable based on what you want out of the negotiation.

✔ **A slur of any kind:** Negative comments about the race, gender, sexual orientation, or national origin of another person are no longer widely tolerated. Some people are offended at any inquiry that could even identify these traits, such as "What kind of a name is that?" Unless you know differently for sure, steer clear of the most innocent of references unless they are relevant.

Even if you're with a group that seems to be quite open about expressing whatever they happen to think or feel about another group, don't join in. You never know who may be suffering in silence — feeling outnumbered and helpless.

The last thing you want in a tough negotiation is to let an offensive phrase slip out just when you want to close. You can lose the deal you are working on *and* the trust and confidence of your counterpart in the negotiation. Unwitting slurs can stop a negotiation in its tracks. You may be pegged forever as a bigot; and some people don't negotiate with bigots. If you have some bad habits in this area, work on cleaning up your language.

Chapter 6

Pushing the Pause Button to Turn Off the Hot Buttons

*T*he ability to maintain emotional distance from whatever is being discussed is what differentiates the master negotiator from the very good or merely lucky negotiator. The best way I know to maintain this emotional distance in a negotiation is through a technique I call *pushing the pause button.* Knowing when and how to push the pause button not only endows you with an aura of composure and confidence, but also gives you control over all the critical points of the negotiation.

This chapter explores the wonderful world of the pause button and the hot buttons that everyone has. The more you know about all these buttons, the better success you will have in negotiating and in life.

Defining the Pause Button

Pushing your pause button is the best way to keep some emotional distance during high-stress situations — at home, at work, anywhere you need a little space. Waiting can be good — doing nothing is sometimes the right action.

Pushing the pause button just means putting the negotiations on hold for a moment or an hour or an evening while you sort things out. You step away, physically or psychologically, to review the work you have done up to that point and check over your plan for the rest of the negotiation.

Pushing the pause button gives you the opportunity to review the entire process of negotiating and to make sure that you aren't overlooking anything. It allows you to avoid getting boxed into a corner. By pushing the pause button, you keep your emotions from ruling (and ruining) the negotiation.

Telling the Other Person that You Need a Pause

Everyone has a different way of pushing the pause button. Sometimes, how you push pause depends on the situation:

- Ask for a night to think the negotiation over. Most people will respect your request to "sleep on it."

- Excuse yourself to the restroom. Who's going to refuse *that* request?

- For a short break, just lean back in your chair and say, "Wait a minute, I have to take that in." For a dramatic touch, try closing your eyes or rubbing your chin.

- Having someone with whom you have to consult before giving a final answer is a convenient excuse for pressing pause. Simply say, "I'll have to run this by my partner (or boss or consultants or whomever) and get back to you at nine tomorrow morning."

So that's the idea: Your pause button is anything you do to create a space so you can think over your next move. In chess, those breaks can take so long that competitive chess has rules about how long the thinking time can be. At the end of the time, a buzzer goes off. In a negotiation, nothing dictates the length of breaks. You have to fight to create the time instead of being forced out of time by an artificial time limit.

Checking with the boss: A classic that needs a little prep

If you plan to consult with your boss as a means of pushing pause in a negotiation, let the other party know that you don't have final say. However, don't use this reason unless you have a boss whom you have to check with from time to time.

Admitting early in the negotiation that you don't have final authority is often beneficial. Make it clear that someone above you must approve the decision. That way, the other party won't get angry with you. Working this information into the beginning of your negotiating formalizes the pause button and sets the tone for a thoughtful, considered negotiation.

Taking notes now for pauses later

Taking notes is helpful at many points in a negotiation, but note taking can also be a pause button. In fact, one of the best times to pull out your pen is when you need to pause. Rather than blurting out an inappropriate or angry response to a confusing or upsetting statement, tell the speaker to hold on while you write it down.

A 9-year-old experiences the pause button

My mother sent me to spend one summer with my Uncle Jim, who lived in Georgia. Quickly, I noticed how cautiously he answered questions to which my mom would give a quick yes. Very often, when I made a request, he would ask a few questions. (I now recognize that he was merely preparing himself because I was a new commodity for him.) If he still was not ready to answer, he would light his pipe!

He would ceremoniously tamp the tobacco in the pipe, ritualistically light it with a long wooden match, and then draw deeply, holding his breath for what seemed like an eternity, before slowly exhaling the thin blue smoke into the silent, anticipatory space. Occasionally, he would go through all the motions again, though I was sure the pipe was lit.

(continued)

(continued)

Whatever followed seemed like wisdom redefined. How clever! The wisdom was not so much in his decision but in my uncle's comfortable and not-so-obvious pushing of the pause button.

Buying even a little time to review and distance oneself from the negotiation is the critical difference between the master negotiator and the merely good negotiator.

Asking the other party to check what you've written to be sure that you got it right can be enormously effective if the words upset you. Seeing their words on paper almost always causes the other party to backtrack, amend, or better yet, erase the words altogether. You'll find that most people don't want their unreasonable statements on paper for all the world to see.

Knowing When to Pause

Use the pause button at each critical moment to review the negotiation or to decide when to close a deal. Definitely use the pause button whenever you are feeling pressured or under stress.

Of course, the pause you take is only as valuable as what you do during it. Ask yourself specific questions during these brief respites. Circumstances differ for every negotiation. Usually, you need to ponder a specific point. You may want to use the time to check over the other five essential skills in a negotiation:

- ✔ **Prepare:** Do you need any additional pieces of information?

- ✔ **Set goals or limits:** How close are you to your original goals? Is the shortfall acceptable? Are the limits you previously set still viable considering the additional information you have gained during the negotiation?

- ✔ **Listen:** Did you hear everything the other person said? Did it match up with the body language? Do you need to go back and ask any questions?

- ✔ **Be clear:** Do you wish you had expressed a point or an idea more clearly or directly? Try to answer this question from your counterpart's point of view, not yours.

> ✔ **Know when to close:** Can any part of the negotiation be closed now? If it seems like everyone is in agreement, have you had plenty of time to live with the final proposal before accepting it?

Sometimes you push pause just to give your mind a break, and sometimes you push pause button for everybody involved, especially if things have gotten a little heated.

Parties can get caught up in the emotions of a negotiation. They're afraid to lose face. They become angry or distrustful of the other party. They fall in love with the deal and ignore facts important to making a decision — especially if the decision ought to be to walk away. They let their own moods, or the moods of the other party, rule the negotiating sessions, causing the negotiations to wander off course. These problems disappear when you use a pause button.

Pausing before a concession

Every request for a concession calls for pushing the pause button. A pause indicates that the concession is significant. Otherwise, the other party doesn't realize he or she has gained anything. No concession is unimportant.

A pause, no matter how slight, before making a concession gives you an opportunity to be sure it's the right thing to do. You want to be sure that you always have something left to give up in order to hold onto what is important to you.

The obvious and easiest example of the dangers of not pushing the pause button before a concession is conceding a price too quickly. Too often, a quick concession robs the other party of the good feelings she rightfully deserves after making a good bargain. Your counterpart may feel that she priced the article too low and that she could have gotten more if she'd been smarter. Although that may be true, what advantage is it to you that she feels that way? None. Worse, now she's out to prevent that mistake from occurring the next time you negotiate, or she compensates by taking a hard line on another aspect of the deal. Giving a concession too quickly can have ramifications across the board.

Pausing under pressure

Some negotiators use pressure to get what they want from you. They may impose an artificial deadline, use emotional "hurry up" language, or ask intimidating questions, such as "Don't you trust me?" or "What else could you possibly need to know?" Don't give in to these pressures. Tell whoever is bullying you into reaching a decision that if you're not allowed to use your pause button, you're not going to negotiate with him at all. Sometimes the pause button is your only defense against being pressured into making a decision based on someone else's deadline.

Decisions made under artificial pressures — especially time pressures imposed by the other side in a negotiation — are often flawed simply because the decision maker does not have sufficient time to consult that most personal of counselors, the inner voice.

If you're being pressured to reach a decision immediately, you can push the pause button to assess whether you need to push the pause button. Take a few moments to consider whether the pressure for a speedy response is reasonable or not.

If You're Not the Only One to Pause

Sometimes you sense that the other person needs to push the pause button. Never say so in so many words. Instead, be very explicit about your need to take a break:

- ✔ "I need a break."
- ✔ "You know, things are getting a little heated in here. Can I take five?"
- ✔ "Let's call it quits for a while. Can we get together tomorrow morning to pick this back up?"

Contrast this non-threatening approach with sentences that use the word "you" a lot. For instance, "Hey, pal, you really need to cool off. Let's take a break." The other party will put up resistance or react negatively to such a statement every time. When you request a pause, focus on your needs and wants.

When someone else asks for a break, be very cautious before you resist it. If a person needs thinking time or needs a moment to regroup, allow it. In fact, take a break yourself. But be alert. If you conclude, after one or two breaks, that the other party is unfocused or is not paying attention, you may decide to try to extend a session. You have to distinguish between the other party using a pause button and the other party just being restless or tired.

Dealing with Your Hot Buttons and Other Emotional Responses

Everybody experiences emotions and responses. Just because you're involved in a negotiation doesn't mean that you'll remain cool, calm, and collected throughout. In fact, the more important the negotiation is to you on a personal level, the more likely it is to stir up your emotional responses.

When you feel emotions welling up inside you, having control means that you choose to use these emotions to your advantage, instead of allowing them to send you to the locker room in defeat or cause you to blow up.

To negotiate masterfully, you must stay in control of your emotions. This means having the confidence to take control in the first place and the skill to channel your emotions effectively as the negotiation progresses. You can usually do this — with one exception: when people or situations push your hot buttons. *Hot buttons* are stimuli that trigger a response of resistance and tempt you to go out of control.

Identifying your hot buttons

So before I go any further, I want you to list your hot buttons. The question is: "What makes your blood pressure rise?" or "When are you most likely to get upset in a negotiation?" Write down your answers.

Acknowledging clearly and unequivocally what upsets you in a negotiation is a big step toward avoiding that situation. You recognize your own demons. You won't get rid of your hot buttons, but you will know to push your pause button as soon as the other party exhibits a certain behavior. Does yelling bother you? If you are aware of that, you can push your pause button at the first sound of a raised voice.

Pushing the pause button on anger

When people don't get what they want, one natural response is to get angry. However, you have the ability to express anger calmly, but firmly. Anger is often useful in helping determine your limits. (Truth be told, you usually get angry because you allowed someone to cross your limits.)

If you don't express your anger, it will find a way to slip out — perhaps in a way that destroys the entire negotiation. You don't let your anger show by going ballistic, however. Instead, consciously and calmly express your anger, using "I" statements. For example, say, "I feel really angry because . . ." Avoid "you" statements such as "You are wrong because . . ." They invariably escalate the emotional charge in the situation.

A prime factor in effective negotiation is the honest communication between the parties. If you are truly angry about something that has happened, you need to tell the other side. People are not mind readers. They don't know when they have stepped over the line unless you tell them. Let some time go by, but don't let the point go, especially if your relationship with the other party matters to you.

Expressing enthusiasm

Many people are afraid that if they reveal how much they want a negotiation to end in their favor, they will be taken advantage of. But as long as you properly prepare and set your limits, you cannot be exploited. In fact, letting others know how much you want what they are selling can give you a great advantage. You can even get the seller to become sympathetic to your position after you reveal how much you want the item in question.

Using anger to reset limits

Not too long ago, I was negotiating the details of a major stage presentation scheduled to appear at one of the leading theaters in Los Angeles, whom I represent. The producer and I had a two-page agreement covering all the big stuff — dates, ticket prices, and such. But we were having a devil of a time with the details.

My client was talking directly with the producer over some technical points. Tempers flared. With a rising voice and a "we'll teach you a lesson" tone, the other party told my client that the production would just bypass Los Angeles altogether. Such a rescheduling would actually have been more convenient for the other side than sticking to their promise to come to Los Angeles on the agreed dates.

After a couple of weeks, things settled down. My client didn't want to "make a stink about it." I convinced him that constructive comment was useful. The next time I talked to the lawyer for the other side, I told her how wrong I thought her client's approach was. I calmly said that threats to break our written agreement really made me angry, that my client was angry as well, and threats had no place in our relationship.

Her initial reaction was the same as my client's: "Oh, that has all blown over. We didn't really mean it." I reiterated my position clearly and firmly. When she tried to minimize it, I told her I wasn't looking for an apology, but I felt I had to stick with the point until I was sure that she understood. By minimizing the situation, she made me think she didn't understand that all of our discussions had to take place on the premise that each side would live up to its commitments in the written (and signed) short-form agreement. She paused, and then said, "I understand."

We never heard such a threat again. We have negotiated more shows with the same company and expect to continue to work with them for years to come.

Note that the first outburst nearly blew the entire negotiation and damaged the relationship. My statement (noting that my client and I were both angry about the way we'd been treated) went a long way to clear the air. Although no one apologized, we reached an understanding, and no more threats were made.

Use these guidelines about expressing enthusiasm during a negotiation:

> ✔ Don't be afraid to show that you really want something . . . that you like it . . . that you think it is terrific . . . that you would do almost anything to own it, and so on.

✔ Always resist the temptation to gloat or make an outburst when you think that you have won a point. *Gloating* is expressing excessive satisfaction and tends to tell your counterpart that you defeated him or her. Gloating suggests to the other side that he or she should not have made the deal. It is better to stay humble (not arrogant) even when you win every point. You don't want your counterparts to feel exploited. Just tell them how much you enjoyed working with them.

Don't let your enthusiasm cause you to promise something that you can't or won't deliver. And when you're negotiating with someone who is very enthusiastic, be sure that any promises he or she makes to you during the course of the negotiation show up in the written contract.

If you have otherwise prepared and set limits, virtually no risk is involved in honestly appreciating the object of the negotiation. You are able to walk away if the terms of the sale are not right.

Employing a positive attitude

Your attitude is the first thing people are exposed to during a negotiation, even before you voice a greeting or reach across the table to shake hands. When you display a *positive attitude* — that is, believing that a situation will turn out favorably — your body language reflects your thoughts and sends signals of openness. (See Chapter 4 for more on body language.)

This idea is critical when you hit a speed bump in the negotiation. In those tough situations, it's not what happens to you that counts. It's how you react to what happens to you. The pause button is a powerful tactic you can use to think and act positively.

Use these four tips to help you maintain a top-notch attitude at the negotiating table:

✔ **Focus on the future rather than on the past.** Focus on where you want to be and what you want to do. Create a clear image of your ideal outcome to the negotiation and then take whatever action you can to begin moving in that direction.

✔ **Focus on the solution.** Whenever you're faced with a problem in the negotiation, focus on what you can do to change it. Don't waste time rehashing and reflecting on the problem. Think and talk about the ideal solution to the setback. Solutions are usually positive, whereas problems tend to be negative. When you offer solutions, you become a positive and constructive person.

✔ **Look for the good.** Assume that something good is hidden within each challenge. The old saying about every cloud having a silver lining contains a lot of truth. If you look for the silver, you will find it. Whenever you push the pause button (see "Defining the Pause Button" earlier in this chapter), you have the opportunity to search for the positive in the situation.

✔ **Look for the valuable lesson.** No matter what comes up in the negotiation, assume that whatever you are facing at the moment is exactly what you need to ultimately be successful. Use it to learn, expand, and grow.

Dealing with discouragement

Many professional negotiators work in the sales field. Selling, even when it's done well, involves a great deal of rejection and failure, which can lead to feelings of frustration and discouragement.

Rather than feeling discouragement or self-pity, consider failure to be a learning experience; that is, failure is really feedback that enables you to change direction. I like to say, "Every 'no' puts you one step closer to 'yes.' Gathering in the 'no's' gets you to the ultimate 'yes'."

Failure is not an accident. Failure has structure and sequence involving people, thoughts, feelings, and actions. Once you understand this sequence, you can work to structure things differently in the future. Failure provides a great learning opportunity; view it as the lifeblood of success.

If things go wrong in a negotiation, don't wait for others to change. Start by changing yourself and turning your failure into an opportunity; the following pointers can help you:

✔ **Get rid of all negative emotions and learn.** There is no failure, only feedback! Briefly acknowledge your discouragement, and then focus on what you could have done differently.

✔ **Go into your next negotiation with a fresh mind-set.**
Use the situation you are in now as a starting point, and
then consider various options as a roadmap to your ultimate success.

✔ **Take different views of the situation.** Consider how the
situation appears to someone who isn't involved. Take
the emotions (yours and your counterpart's) out of the
picture, and then think about how both parties inter-
acted and try to better understand the process.

In a protracted negotiation, you must be prepared to face
frustration again and again. Anything worth doing has the
potential for triggering a great deal of frustration.

Handling Stressful Situations

Stress is an internal response to an external event. All the
people and situations in a negotiation make up the *external*
event, and all your mental and physical reactions (including
stress) are *internal* responses. Because the external events
seldom are under your complete control, how can you change
your internal response? The next sections offer some pointers.

At WAR with yourself

There you are — in the same negotiation . . . again. A few
people are stubbornly saying the same things they said last
week, and you can't see any progress. "I hate being here,"
you begin to think. You start to worry about being late to
your next appointment. Your face feels hot, and your temple
starts to throb. Just then, someone says something about the
computers being down (again) and that's why the new figures
aren't ready yet. On top of it all, the room is terribly warm
and, remember, you're never supposed to let them see you
sweat. "These people don't know how to control the temperature," you think, glaring at strangers across the table. You feel
your neck and shoulders tighten, and the throb in your right
temple intensifies and spreads across your forehead. "My day
is ruined," your internal voice declares. And it may be.

Stress is caused by resisting what's going on around you.
When you resist a stalled negotiation, a rude person, or an
uncomfortable situation, you respond with three emotions:
worry, anger, and resentment. The first letters of these three

words describe the stress response perfectly: WAR; that is, the war within you. Applying each to this stalled negotion:

- ✔ **Worry:** You worry about being late. Are you going to a beloved, joy-filled place or to a place you'd rather not go, where you feel anxiety and pressure to perform? What's the worry really about — fear of reprisal or punishment? Is it perceived lack of choice on your part?

- ✔ **Anger:** You feel anger at people you suspect aren't hearing you. Is the suspicion familiar? Do you often mistrust people — and yourself? Or is your anger related to the notion that you do more than most people and aren't properly recognized for your effort? Do you feel the duties you have in life are fairly distributed, or do you feel you do more than your share? Many external events can bring this anger to the surface.

- ✔ **Resentment:** You feel resentment at these people who don't know how to control the temperature in their own office! Are you often impatient with people who don't do things exactly as you do?

Realize that your emotions are not a part of the event itself; the event is merely the trigger that sets off these emotions *inside* you. Try to distinguish the emotions from the events.

Your emotions are human and normal. You gain control when you are aware of your emotions. When you ignore the WAR, the stress and tension build up inside of you. Awareness puts you in charge of your reactions.

Stop, look, and listen . . . before you have a meltdown

When you feel stressed out, seething over what would be minor irritations in a different situation, stop and take a look at your reaction. You may be feeling worried, angry, and resentful all at once. Consider the opposite of this reaction — acceptance. Don't think, "Oh goody, a stalled negotiation!" Instead, think about recognition, such as, "Ah — a stalled negotiation. That's one of the things that drives me crazy, and now I must deal with it." Use humor to accept your circumstances.

Only when you accept a situation can you effectively act upon it. If you're busy resisting it, you're paralyzed.

Acceptance involves three steps:

✔ **Stop:** Push the pause button. You can use it to gain control over an automatic emotional response. (See "Knowing When to Pause" earlier in this chapter.)

✔ **Look:** Recognize that you are now experiencing one of your stress triggers. Then recognize that you can choose whether to get upset. *Look* also means to look at what you really want and ask, "Is being emotional going to help me get it?" Usually, the answer is no.

✔ **Listen:** Pay attention to what your inner self is telling you to do. Generally, if you don't like the deal you're being handed in a negotiation, you have three alternatives: adapt, alter, or avoid.

• *Adapt* means adapting yourself to the situation. Listen to what the person is saying. You may have unrealistic expectations about the time it takes your counterpart to reach a resolution, and you may have to adapt to a delay.

• *Alter* means changing the situation. Find alternative routes to your goal; prepare better before the negotiation starts.

• *Avoid* can usually be eliminated right away. Unless you avoid negotiations altogether, you can't avoid people and situations that may cause you to be overly emotional.

The best tool to handle emotional people is the empathetic statement. A sincerely empathetic statement shows that you're listening. Listening by making an empathetic statement defuses emotional people because often such people are being emotional to make their points heard. The *empathetic statement* is calming, comforting, positive, and specific. A good one takes only six seconds. "I understand how frustrating it is not to get the information when you want it." Six seconds. "I understand how easy it is to get impatient with that machine." Six seconds. "It sounds like you're very upset. It looks like you need our full cooperation." Six seconds. Not only do you defuse the other person, you now have time to think of a response to achieve your goal while staying within your limits.

Chapter 7

Closing the Deal and Feeling Good About It

. . . .

In This Chapter

▶ Exposing the facts and myths about win-win negotiating

▶ Recognizing what constitutes a win

▶ Finding creative solutions

▶ Bringing closure to a deal

. . . .

*T*his chapter is about the glory moment when it all comes together — when you close the deal. It's also about closing the deal in a way that makes both sides feel good about the outcome. A deal closes when the parties agree on enough terms that they can move forward with the performance of the deal.

Most people think of closing the deal as the only satisfactory resolution of a negotiation. However, it's critical to figure out *whether* the deal should close and, if so, how to close it to ensure smooth performance throughout the life of the agreement. This chapter covers the skills and techniques of actually closing the deal so that it will last and — if necessary — how to walk out if there is no deal to be made.

Closing is a skill that you must develop separately — and keep in mind every step of the way — if you are to become a successful negotiator. Use your closing skills from the first moment of the negotiation.

Good Deals, Bad Deals, and Win-Win Negotiating

A *win-win solution,* a deal in which both sides are satisfied, is what you aim for. But you won't know if you're winning unless you can tell the difference between a good deal and a bad deal. That situation should never be the case if you use this book.

- ✔ A *good deal* is one that is fair under all circumstances at the time the agreement is made. It provides for various contingencies before problems arise. A good deal is workable in the real world.

  Be sure that the other side agrees that the deal is a good one. You don't want to sign a deal with someone who is harboring resentments over some aspect of the agreement.

- ✔ A *bad deal* is not fair under all the circumstances. It allows foreseeable events to create problems in the relationship after the deal is struck. Some aspect of the agreement looks great on paper but simply doesn't work out in the real world — for reasons that were predictable during the deal-making process.

What is and isn't fair is very subjective. You determine whether a deal is good or bad for you; the other party does the same from his or her perspective.

Assessing the deal

To be sure that you have a good deal and a win-win situation, take a break just before closing (push the pause button — see Chapter 6). Ask yourself the following questions:

- ✔ Do you know the person you're dealing with and why he or she wants to make this deal with you?

- ✔ Based on all the information, can the other side perform the agreement to your expectations?

- ✔ Does this agreement further your personal long-range goals? Does the outcome of the negotiation fit into your own vision statement?

> ✔ Does this agreement fall comfortably within the goals and the limits you set for this particular negotiation?
>
> ✔ Are the people on both sides who have to carry out the agreement fully informed and ready to do what it takes to make the deal work?

In the ideal situation, the answer to all of these questions is a resounding *yes*. If you are unsure about any one of them, take some extra time to review the entire situation. Assess how the agreement could be changed to create a *yes* answer to each question and try your best to make the changes needed.

When you have a yes response to each question, close the deal. Don't go for any more changes even if you think that the other person wouldn't mind — you never know!

Justify your decision to yourself

If you can't alter the deal so that you can answer yes to each question above, think carefully before closing. If you decide to go forward, write down exactly why you are closing the deal despite some reservations. This exercise is particularly helpful to your state of mind if the results don't work out — you have a record as to why you took the deal. You won't be so hard on yourself.

Get more information

If you have a question about the answer to any of the first three questions, get more information either from the other side or from another source. Ask people who may know about the other person open-ended questions that seek a true opinion. (Go to Chapter 3 for advice on asking questions.)

The people you deal with are more important than the paperwork you draft. Know your counterpart very well before you enter into a long-term relationship. No lawyer can protect you from a crook, and no matter how strong your case is, you don't want to be in a lawsuit.

Don't backtrack

Going back for one more little item that's not all that important may annoy the other side and threaten the entire deal. No one wants to do business with someone who wastes time trying to grab some small, additional advantage instead of closing up the deal and moving on when it's time to do so.

Creating win-win deals

Some negotiations are pretty straightforward, and the interests of each party are clear. In more complicated negotiations, the motivations are not always so easy to find, at least not the more subtle factors that are driving the negotiation. Sometimes some head scratching and imagination is required to fully understand the interests of the other side.

In my seminars, I like to present a negotiating problem adapted from a story from the Middle East that dates back to the seventh century:

> A wise Arab left 19 camels to his three sons. To the oldest, he left half of his camels. To the middle son, he left a third. To the youngest, he left a sixth. Unfortunately, 19 does not divide by any of the fractions that dear old dad mentioned in his will.
>
> The three sons quarreled long into the night. (*Quarreling* is unartful negotiating.) One wanted to own the camels communally. One wanted to sell the camels and split the profit. One just wanted to go to sleep. Finally, they consulted with the wise woman of the village. What did she tell them?

Here's is a hint to the solution: This wise woman is smart enough to know that she ought to charge these three lads for solving their problem. She told the three young men to give her one camel as a fee, and the payment would solve the problem. The oldest son took his half of the camels (9), the middle son took his third (6), and the youngest took his sixth (3). The negotiation was a real win-win because the three brothers lived happily ever after, and the wise old woman had new stature in the village.

This is a great story, but it comes with a caution: The wise woman's solution only worked because the brothers wanted to close the deal in a way that was fair among them. If any one of them was seeking an exact, legal interpretation of the father's will, this solution was nothing more than a mathematical trick.

Concessions versus Conditions

In a negotiation, you make concessions and conditions, so you need to understand the difference between the two. A *concession* is when you give up a point. Don't forget to get something back for it. A *condition* is what you require to grant the concession. For instance, you might say, "I would be willing to knock 20 percent off the price if you can guarantee an order of this size each month for the next three months." The condition is a guarantee of additional sales. If the other side purchases only the original amount and refuses to give you that concession, it must pay full price.

Always keep the concession/condition balance in mind during a negotiation. You can put a condition on any concession that you are willing to give during a negotiation. In fact, you should receive some specific benefit for each concession.

You can view each request for a concession as a mini-negotiation within the larger negotiation. You give in order to get. But always consider what you can ask for in return. Be stingy with your concessions; they are the coins of the various transactions that take place during a negotiation.

Don't make any concessions until you have a sense of everything that the other side will demand. You don't want to reach the end of the negotiation having given up everything you could give up without receiving everything that you wanted to receive.

As you negotiate concessions and conditions, try using phrases such as "Assuming we reach agreement on everything else, . . ." or "As long as the overall deal works, . . ." This statement helps you and your counterpart make sure everyone gets what they want.

Understanding the Letter of the Law

A short course on contract law is well beyond the scope of this book, but you should understand a few key points if you ever negotiate a deal in the business world. These short sections won't make you a lawyer or eliminate the need for a lawyer, but they will make you savvier about the negotiating you do.

Legal definition of a closed deal

Unless you have a specific arrangement to the contrary, no deal is closed until the parties reach an agreement on all the points under negotiation. As long as some point is under discussion, the deal remains open and subject to adjustment by either party. That is the way U.S. law works.

Even if an agreement seems to be in place regarding various pieces of the deal, the deal isn't final until both parties reach an agreement on all points. Backing off on previously agreed-to points doesn't happen often, but it does happen, even to experienced negotiators.

To have an enforceable contract, you need agreement on four elements:

✓ What you are getting

✓ What you are paying for what you are getting

✓ How long the contract will last

✓ Who the parties are in the contract

Everything else, you can work out along the way. If you are missing any one of those four items, you cannot have an enforceable contract.

Offers and counteroffers

When a party makes an offer and you make a counteroffer, the law looks at the transaction in a very particular way. Legally, you rejected the initial offer and put a new offer on the table. The other party may allow you to accept a previous offer, but is not bound to do so. You do not have a legal right to demand that the old offer from the other side stay on the table after you have rejected it and put another offer on the table.

Written versus oral contracts

Contrary to popular belief, oral agreements are generally enforceable. The law requires a few contracts to be in writing: Some examples are contracts that sell land, employment contracts for one year or longer, and contracts that convey an interest in a copyright. But generally, contracts do not have to be in writing.

The problem is with proving the contents of an oral agreement. If you get into a dispute, be assured that you and the other side will remember the agreement differently. The situation can be pretty hopeless unless you have something other than your own memory that hints at the terms of the contract.

Legal protection before the contract

It's fine if one or both parties begin to carry out the terms of the deal before a fully enforceable contract is signed. The courts won't abandon someone who acted in good faith. Worst case: The party who performed the service or provided the goods will receive the fair market value for that service or product. This concept is called *quantum meruit.* (There — I did it. I got a Latin phrase in the book!) Literally, that ancient phrase means "what the thing is worth."

Recognizing When to Close

Keep the closing in mind as you prepare for your negotiation, as you listen to the other side, and every time you speak. A little piece of your mind should always focus on the closing — on bringing the negotiation to a mutually acceptable solution. The proper moment to make your first effort at closing a deal is when you first sit down.

Your mantra for closing: early and often. A recent study of salespeople revealed that a very small percentage of sales close after the first effort. Most sales close after at least three efforts to get the order.

If you have trouble closing deals, intentionally try to close your next negotiation earlier than you think is possible. You find that no harm is done and that the other side actually becomes sensitized to the need to conclude matters. Your rate of successful closings rises as you become more and more aware of closing as a separate skill to bring out early and often.

Many people find it is easier to close a deal if they set a deadline to do so. Negotiations tend to fall into place at the last minute. Every deal has time constraints, so establishing a deadline can help the negotiation come to a smooth end.

The phony deadline is a classic negotiating tool used to hurry one side into a quick close. If you suspect a phony deadline, test it. Get an explanation.

Knowing How to Close

With a friend or family member, rehearse the various approaches for closing I explain in the next sections. The more naturally they roll off your tongue, the easier the attempt will be for you in a real situation. Role play. Describe a typical negotiation situation to a friend and then have your friend challenge you with the objections in this section.

Push the pause button before closing (I explain the pause button in Chapter 6). Take a breather, look over the entire agreement. Make sure it works for you and the other side in the real world. In fact, when you use the six essential skills described in Chapter 1, somebody at the negotiating table almost certainly figures out how to close up the deal if it's truly ready to be closed. If everyone at the table is using these basics, you are likely to close the deal much more quickly.

The good closer

People who resolve conflicts and solve problems in their personal lives are thought of as agreeable and cooperative. At the negotiating table, they're considered brilliant. When a negotiator finds a solution to what appears to be a difficult negotiation, he or she earns praise all around — including from the folks on the other side of the table. More than once, people I faced across the negotiating table have asked me to represent them in an unrelated negotiation.

Characteristics of strong and weak closers:

- ✔ **Strong closers always seem to find a solution.** The approach may not be the original one, but it gets the desired result. Weak closers tend to get stuck on a position.

- ✔ **Strong closers generally accomplish tasks on time.** Weak closers often procrastinate in many aspects of their lives.

- ✔ **Strong closers rejoice when a deal closes.** Weak closers feel either a sense of loss when the project comes to an end or waves of self-doubt. Either way, closing does not bring unbridled joy to the weak closer in the same way it does for the strong closer.

Good closers are often witty or clever, but they don't have to be. They just need to have the confidence to follow through with the goals and limits they set when they started planning the negotiation. Creating consensus where none exists is a fun activity for the good closer and a struggle for the weak closer.

The only three closing strategies you'll ever need

The entire country seems to be in a search of the perfect close — the one that won't fail. When I get to this point in my seminars, pencils are poised. Fresh paper is found. The class is alert. Here's the big secret: The three ways to make the sale or to successfully close the negotiation are

1. Ask

2. Ask

3. Ask

No matter how powerful your computer is, what the range of your cell phone is, or how clever your tracking system is, you still have just one way to get the order or close the deal: Ask whether your counterpart will agree to the current terms.

Using linkage to close

Linkage is a great concept to help close a deal when no compromise is in sight on the last point in contention. *Linkage* simply means that you hook a requested concession to something you want so the deal can close.

This situation cries out for a linkage strategy:

- ✔ The parties on the other side are making a final demand. They can't go any further. They can't give any more than they already have.

- ✔ You don't want to cave in on this point, because the deal won't work for you. If you concede, you won't have enough incentive to close the deal.

Here is what you do:

1. **Take a pause.**

   Be sure that the other side is not just bluffing, that they really can't go any further on this point.

2. **Look over the entire transaction. Find an area where you didn't get everything you wanted or find an item that can be changed in your favor to bring balance back to the deal.**

3. **Link the two issues together.**

   Tell the other side that you will agree to their request if they will make the adjustment you need.

   The item you link may never have been discussed before or, more likely, it was discussed, and you tentatively agreed to drop your desire. But linkage is always acceptable. It makes you the creative problem solver.

The other side wants the deal to close just as much as you do. When you bring balance to your side without throwing the other side out of balance, everyone gets something they want. You are a genius. At least, that's what people will say.

Common phrases used to introduce the linkage concept include

"Well, maybe we could look at some of the issues again."

"Well, we may be able to work something out here."

"Tell ya what I'm gonna do."

Linkage is one of those tools that makes you feel like a real top-notch negotiator, because it helps you solve a real problem. Neither side can give on the point under discussion, so you find something to trade. Use linkage to find your way out of a tough spot, the next time you find yourself in one.

Barriers to Closing

If you find it difficult to close, the real question is probably not "How do I do this?" but rather "Why do I hesitate instead of going for it?" Merely stating the question helps you to start thinking about the answer.

Overcoming fears

Each person who has a barrier to closing a negotiation or a sale probably has some fears or apprehensions about the process. The most common fears are

- **Fear of failure:** Most people have this fear to one extent or another. In extreme cases, this fear keeps you from asking for what you want. After all, if you don't ever make your request, you can never fail to get it.

- **Fear of rejection:** Everybody wants to be loved. Nobody likes being cast aside. If you don't ask for an agreement, you won't be rejected. It can be as simple as that.

- **Fear of criticism:** Some people work in a situation in which they are likely to be criticized no matter what favorable the agreement. One way to prevent those negative words and looks is to never close the deal. Who can criticize a deal while it's still being negotiated?

- **Fear of making a mistake:** Some people believe that making a mistake is a sin instead of a normal part of life. So instead of finalizing a deal that may not be perfect, these people shy away from closing the negotiation.

✔ **Fear of commitment:** Closing a deal is a powerful commitment. Sometimes closing a deal triggers a short-term commitment with longer-term consequences (such as buying a car); Sometimes closing a deal results in a commitment that requires participation on both sides for longer than most American marriages last. It's no surprise that many people get hung up on making a commitment.

✔ **Fear of loss:** Some negotiations last a long time and can be pretty intense. Closing the negotiation means losing that intense relationship.

You can minimize the impact of such fears, even if you don't purge them completely from your system. One of the following tips may work for you:

✔ **Keep in mind the consequences of not going for the close.** When you don't try to close, you end up in the same position as if you had been rejected. You put yourself exactly where you don't want to be.

✔ **Think about the criticism you'll receive from those who are looking to you to close this deal.**

✔ **Put words to your fear.** You can actually tell the other side the problem, such as, "Here's the hard part for me. I need to close this deal or call it quits."

✔ **Put a deadline on the negotiation up front and talk about it with the other side.** That way, even the person on the other side of the table will be helping you.

The other party may have some mental blocks to closing also. If you sense that the person you are negotiating with has a fear that is blocking a close, use one of the techniques in the preceding list — set a time frame for the negotiation, mention the folks who want the other side to close the deal, or mention the consequences of not closing the deal.

Overcoming objections

When someone directly states an objection to whatever you are proposing, an opportunity is at hand. You have the opportunity to clear away one more barrier and get closer to your goal of closing the negotiation. An objection — honestly stated — is just another way of inviting you to satisfy some concern or to meet a need that you didn't address earlier.

Countering objections is the part where you get to show your stuff, and your preparation really pays off because you get to explain why. Answering objections is the fun part of a negotiation.

Using questions to get where you want to go

When you try to close a negotiation and you get an objection, a question is your best friend. Gently probe to find the answers to the following:

- ✔ Is the stated objection really the thing that is bothering the other party?

- ✔ What will the other party do if this deal doesn't close? What is his or her *or else?* (Go to Chaper 2 for more on limits.)

- ✔ Can you meet or beat that alternative?

The frustrating dilemma is that you cannot state these questions in a direct manner. You must ask for the information indirectly. For example, you usually can't say, "Come on, tell me what's really bugging you." You have to relax yourself and get the other party to relax so you can get to the source of the concern. Try these ways to tickle out the information (each question is a variation on the theme):

- ✔ "If we can find agreement on that one item can we close this deal today?" If not, you know something else is bothering the other person.

- ✔ "How about if we . . . ?" Suggest a whole new approach. Use linkage to make the deal work for the other party. (When that works, you know that you've stumbled on what is really bothering the other side.)

- ✔ "In a perfect world, what would this deal look like to you?"

You are inside the negotiation, so you have made some progress. The answers to these questions can turn up all sorts of information you need to know — information you can't ask about directly. Keep digging until you're satisfied that you fully understand the objection. (To improve the questions you ask throughout the negotiation, check out Chapter 3.)

Going back to square one

If you run into a blank wall, you may be inclined to shrug your shoulders and say dejectedly, "Well, I guess we're back at square one."

Square one in negotiating is preparation. When you have a hard time with an objection or can't close the negotiation, you generally need more information about the person you're negotiating with, about your own company or product, or about the competition.

When the Deal Is Done

The negotiation is over. The contract is signed. The client is happy. You are being roundly congratulated. Administrative details have yet to be set up, but your job is over — almost.

You have two things left to do for the good of the deal and for your own growth. One is to review the entire negotiation, and the other is to be sure the deal is properly executed. And then the congratulations can begin.

Review the process

As soon as you have a chance to do so, go to a quiet place and think back over the negotiation and consider what you may have done differently. Consider the consequences of the various choices you made. I'm not talking about self-flagellation; I'm talking about calm review of the entire negotiating history, mentally playing out various options you had along the way. This process is one final review after you have time and distance from the completed negotiation. This is particularly useful after the successful negotiation, because you don't have any self-doubt or blame.

Some questions to think about during the review:

- ✔ What additional information could you have gathered before the negotiation started? Where would you have gotten that information?

- ✔ Did you know as much as you would have liked to about the other party?

✔ Were you as well informed as you needed to be about the marketplace?

✔ Were your goals appropriate to the situation? Note that you are not asking if you achieved all your goals. If it happens that you did achieve all your goals, you probably didn't set them high enough.

✔ Were your limits appropriate to the situation? Did you learn anything during the negotiation that caused you to change your limits? Did you adjust your limits to keep the deal instead of adjusting your limits based on new information?

✔ Did you listen as well as you could have? Were there times where you did not have the patience to hear the other side out?

✔ Were you as clear as you could have been throughout the negotiation? Did your lack of clarity ever threaten the deal?

✔ How often did you use your pause button? What pause button did you use? What was happening that caused you to use your pause button?

✔ Did you start closing right away? How many efforts to close did you make?

Set up systems for checking the system

Regardless of whether you are a part of a large organization or negotiate on your own behalf, don't close up the file and consider a negotiation over until you have taken steps to ensure that the agreement will be carried out. You need to make sure that the agreement's execution is ethical, timely, and honest. Precautions you can take include such items as marking a calendar with the dates that various items are due, checking that the people who must carry out the agreement are on board and understand the terms, and making sure that the progress is being reported to the other side.

Most large organizations have a separate department often called Contract Administration or something very close. Even when departmental staff handles these details, you should call the department after an appropriate amount of time has passed (usually a week or two) and satisfy yourself that the servicing system is in place. If you are a salesperson, you want to be sure that the order is being or has been processed.

You check because if something goes wrong in servicing a contract, the problem reflects badly on you. This is true regardless of how far such matters are from your responsibility. You negotiated the deal. If the terms are not carried out in a professional and timely manner, the other party will remember that the deal he or she made with *you* went sour. Unfair, but true.

Make it your personal responsibility to be sure that the other party is happy. The benefits of repeat business for you and the preservation of your own good reputation will benefit you many times over. Your personal duty is to live up to the spirit and letter of the agreement. I consider this a sacred trust. Your word is your bond. Don't ever forget that.

Remember to celebrate!

New beginnings and final endings are celebrated in every culture, even though the events may look very different. No matter where you are in the world, people celebrate reaching important agreements. Some go to church, others throw a party, and some light a candle. A parade occurs almost spontaneously when a surrender is signed to end a war.

The signing ceremony to mark the end of the negotiation and the beginning of the life of the agreement looms large in the United States. Such events feel like a natural time to celebrate. Such celebrations make reopening any discussion on the terms mighty difficult. Americans shake hands even over the smallest agreements and pop champagne corks for the big ones.

It is also important to celebrate when you decide not to close a deal and to walk away from it. Close only a good deal. Avoid the bad deals. Be happy when you do not close a bad deal. Walking away from bad deals is like avoiding a collision in traffic. You breathe a huge sigh of relief and thank goodness that you avoided the accident. When you are successful in avoiding a bad deal, celebrate whatever way you know and love best — but celebrate.

Chapter 8

When the Deal Just Won't Seem to Close

· ·

In This Chapter

▶ Dealing with glitches that block the deal from closing

▶ Handling conflict so both sides benefit

▶ Walking away from a deal

▶ Contemplating a renegotiation

· ·

*Y*ou can get ridiculously close to an agreement, and the entire negotiation can still fall apart on you. After all of the hard work and time you've invested in getting to the final stages, it's frustrating to walk away from the negotiating table empty-handed. This chapter explores the roadblocks, from dirty tricks used by the other party to environmental glitches, that keep a deal from closing and how you can overcome them.

Many circumstances and events can send the best of negotiations skidding off track. In chess, these moves are called gambits. In track, such barriers are hurdles. In steeple chasing, they are hedgerows. In a crime chase, they are roadblocks. In the military, they are Catch 22s. In a negotiation, they are glitches — from the German word, *glitchen,* meaning a slippery spot in the road.

Overcoming the Glitches

Glitches happen. You cannot ignore them or be overly frustrated by them. You can't avoid them. They are part of the life of any negotiator. Heck, they are part of *life.* If you are prepared for them, you actually derive a certain pleasure from dealing with glitches when they come up in a negotiation.

The best way to get through your next glitch is to push the pause button (see Chapter 6). Take a mental break from the negotiation. Check your own performance on the essential skills I outline in Chapter 1. Use that pause button with a vengeance. Find the problem and fix it. Then you can get back to the substance of the negotiation and close the deal. Always keep the negotiation moving toward the desired end.

The sections in this chapter provide general guidelines and some easy steps for getting past some of the most common glitches that people run into when they are negotiating.

Dirty Tricks That Torment

If you make a mistake, the error is easy enough to correct. The frustrations — the glitches — arise from something the *other* party does. It's easy enough to take care of your own goofs. Figuring out your counterpart's goofs and how to get around them takes special talent. Some of the more common, maddening moments in a negotiation are listed in the following sections.

A constant change of position

Any negotiation involves concessions. Each side makes concessions based on the information the two sides exchange about the factual matters and the priorities of the parties. Barring unusual circumstances, priorities should not change. Keep a consistent position about those items that are important to you and what your goals are.

If the other side changes its position concerning what is and what is not important, stop everything until you find out what happened. Don't ignore the issue. One of the following situations occurs:

  ✔ Maybe the other party experienced a significant change of circumstances. Get the new situation firmly in mind. Then revisit the point on which you thought there was some level of agreement. Maybe the new situation calls for a new solution.

> ✔ Perhaps the other side is trying to pull a fast one.
>
> ✔ Maybe the other side is not as prepared as he or she should be. If that's the case, take a break. Your negotiation will go better for both sides if both sides are prepared. Just say, "Maybe we should take this up tomorrow. That will give you time to meet and sort out any last-minute items. No rush. We want you to be ready for this."

Written memos are useful tools in this situation, but a caveat is in order. If a constant change of position is part of a person's negotiating style, expect the person to constantly lose your documentation, not have time to read it, to misplace it, or simply to ignore it.

If you suspect that your counterpart may conveniently lose your written documentation, be sure to use firm and clear language in your memo: "If you disagree with any portion of this memo, please advise by such-and-such a date." Being this specific helps more than saying "as soon as possible" or "immediately," which mean different timeframes to different people. Even more helpful is to distribute your memos to everyone the negotiator wants to impress. This way, the negotiator's peers, superiors, and colleagues can monitor the progress of the proceedings.

Good cop, bad cop

A less obvious but equally dangerous glitch is the good cop/ bad cop ploy. This label grows out of the police interrogation technique of having one officer question a suspect harshly and another, gentler cop be the relief questioner. The gentler cop — the *good cop* — pretends to befriend the suspect. The theory is that the suspect will spill the beans to the good cop.

Don't fall in love with the good cop. The good cop, more often than the bad cop, does you in. If you doubt that, remember that the good cop is the knowing partner of the bad cop. One does not exist without the other. They don't wander unknowingly down different paths. They do what they do deliberately. The good cop is usually the more pleasant personality of the two, but in a negotiating context, they are in cahoots.

Use these ideas for putting the good cop/bad cop duo in their place:

✔ **Use their little game against them.** Go ahead and confide in the good cop. Confide to the good cop that the bad cop has just about blown the deal. Confide about your other opportunities. But never drop your guard. Set deadlines. Be clear. Don't lose focus. Your discussion with the good cop is an extension of your discussion with the bad cop. Don't forget that for one minute.

✔ **Create a bad cop of your own.** Tell your counterparts that you'd love to do what they want, but your boss is obsessed with sticking to the points at hand. It's easier to create your own fictitious bad cop who appears more unyielding than to have a bad cop who is present at the negotiation.

✔ **Let the other team's bad cop talk and talk and talk.** Sometimes it resolves the problem, especially if the bad cop is being obnoxious. Eventually his own team will get tired of hearing him and tell him to quit talking.

✔ **Turn the good cop into a bad cop by calling him on his bluff.** This tells the other side that you're aware of the good cop/bad cop dynamic. Sometimes just identifying them both in your own mind allows you to better handle the situation without having to come out and accuse them.

The invisible partner

One of the more frustrating glitches you can run into in a negotiation is to discover — usually late in the game — that the other side can't agree to anything without consulting some invisible or unavailable partner or boss. Overcoming this glitch can be like shadow-boxing.

If you run into the invisible-partner glitch, you may not have gathered enough information about the other party. You should have determined the decision-making authority of your counterpart early in the negotiation. To a large extent, good preparation avoids the problem of the invisible partner.

The invisible partner is quite similar to the good cop/bad cop tactic, and a bit more frustrating. An unnamed, unseen bad cop is off in the wings continually vetoing the progress made in the discussions. This situation usually arises in small business transactions or real estate deals, although a variation of it can exist in large organizations. Banks often use the so-called loan committee in this way.

If you sense a silent-partner excuse coming, ask for the opportunity to pay your respects to that silent partner — no negotiating. Heavens no, wouldn't think of it. You just want to introduce yourself and pay a courtesy call.

Keep your word. Don't use the first meeting to negotiate, if you promised not to pursue a business discussion. After you have made a courtesy contact, however, you always have the option of making direct contact for the purpose of breaking a logjam. Someone else in your organization can contact the silent partner as well. Frequently, these folks in the wings work behind the scenes because they are really softies and have a hard time saying no themselves. You can use this vulnerability to your advantage.

There is a very helpful, non-negotiating, procedural question that you can ask of the invisible partner, even in the initial meeting. Upon meeting Ivan the Invisible, express your gratitude for having the opportunity to meet him; then assure him that you're delighted to be working with the Designated Negotiator. After the small talk, innocently ask Ivan whether they have had sufficient time to discuss the negotiating parameters. Can you close a deal with the Designated Negotiator? Does Ivan need to be alone with the Designated Negotiator to talk out any more limitations before you and he go further?

You may not be negotiating, but the more you can do to close off this frustrating technique of an invisible authority figure doing you in at every turn, the happier you are and the more smoothly the negotiation goes.

If you are not successful in meeting Ivan the Invisible, try insisting that the invisible partner be in a nearby room or available by telephone during the next negotiation session. Then, if a question arises that requires his or her approval, the other side can't use the absence as an excuse for prolonging the negotiation. You need to prevent delays during the negotiation when you reach the point of conclusion.

Finally, you can always treat the other side's need to get approval from the invisible partner like any other request in a negotiation. The other side usually presents this step as an unavoidable fact of life, but if the negotiation has progressed to the very final stages, I view the invisible partner (or the boss who suddenly needs to approve the deal) as a new request. I then state a similar condition: "Okay, but be sure your partner (or boss) understands that you and I have negotiated this deal to its conclusion. If she changes something, I will have to go back to my people, and they will undoubtedly want to change something. Right now, this deal is acceptable. We have given up some things, and you have given up some things. The deal is in balance. Changing something at this late date could throw it out of whack. It would definitely hold things up."

Such a speech often stops the other party from ever going to Ivan the Invisible. When the other side still insists on consulting with the invisible partner even after my speech, the deal comes back unchanged more often than not.

The double message

Always stay in step with yourself. By this, I mean keeping your words and your actions consistent. Nothing, but nothing, is a bigger barrier to communication than the double message. Some common double messages you may have received in your negotiating experience:

- The threat to break off a negotiation, but the negotiation continues uninterrupted. This behavior baffles the listener.

  This inconsistency will throw into question every future statement the person makes.

- Not mentioning an issue at all during the first negotiating sessions and then making it the most important item on the table.

  This double message is a quite common syndrome I call the "Wimp/Monster." Sometimes people are afraid or don't have time to raise an issue, so they "wimp out." They fail to bring the issue to the table. When they finally raise the issue, it's not well received because it is put on the table so late in the discussion, so they get very upset and turn into a "monster." The better practice is to get all the issues on the table as early as possible.

A common double message occurs when the boss negotiates a task to be done on an immediate, high-priority basis. The job is completed on time and is on the boss's desk at the requested moment — where it sits untouched for the next two weeks. Whoever pulled off the miracle must be acknowledged immediately. Otherwise, the person may be turned off the next time they are told that a similar miracle is needed. After all, the last time a big deal was made about a rush job, the project was not important enough to warrant a comment, even though it was accomplished at breakneck speed. More bosses should recognize these workplace situations for the negotiations they are. This common mistake made with a subordinate would probably not be made with an opponent in an important negotiation.

Nickel and diming

Just when you thought that everything was settled, the person on the other side wants just a few little concessions. Sometimes the requests come at the end of the negotiating session. Sometimes the person asks in a phone call the next morning. Whenever it happens, you're bound to be annoyed. In many cultures, such behavior is accepted, and in other cultures, it's expected. But in America, we think of this type of person as being cheap or chintzy. It is certainly not classy. You should not seek a few more things at the end of a negotiation, and you certainly don't want this to happen to you.

But sooner or later, someone will try to nickel and dime you. Here's how you can respond:

- ✔ Push your pause button (see Chapter 6). A quick count of 1-2-3 might do the trick.
- ✔ Ask a polite question or two to help you find out why this is happening.

Your counterpart may be nickel and diming you because of

- ✔ **Habit:** This person likes to feel that he or she got something for nothing. He asks for a free tie when he buys a suit, usually while the tailor is pinning up the pants.
- ✔ **Buyer's remorse:** After sleeping on it, the other person feels he or she got a bad deal in some way and wants to make it up.

Your first response is to ask questions. Find out where the request is coming from. Often a boss has chewed out the person on the opposite side of the table for not getting some small item (probably the only thing his or her boss knows anything about). Sometimes it is a forgotten item. You want to go over this ground, so that you can ask the most important question of all: "Are sure this is it? Are you positive you won't be coming back for anything more?" After you have all the information you can acquire, you can agree to the request or deny the request.

- ✔ If the request seems legitimate, give the person what he or she requested because it amounts to so little in relation to the entire deal. But don't forget that the person made the request because he or she will probably do it to you again. When you agree to the request, make a big deal out of giving what is asked, and be sure it closes the deal. Tell the person, "It will be in the memo I send over for you to sign," so he or she understands that the concession is tied to closing the deal.

- ✔ If the request is made out of habit and is just an annoyance, turn it down with something like "Sorry, too late." Meet a renewed request with chuckle to underscore the humor in the situation and say something like "Does this really work? Gee, I want to go shopping with you," (without agreeing to make the concession). I sometimes make some lame excuse such as the initial paperwork has already been sent into the system and can't be retrieved, or I just keep repeating something like, "Nope, nope — too late — we closed this up."

"Let's split the difference and be done"

The concept of splitting the difference is one of the most seductive negotiating ploys, but if someone suggests it to you, measure the result. Sometimes people begin a negotiation with a number that is unrealistically high just to impress a counterpart with the size of the subsequent discounts as the bargaining proceeds. If you have been more than fair in your approach, splitting the difference is not necessarily equitable. If the result is unsatisfactory, you need to say so. Don't be afraid of being called a *spoiler* by the other side.

Here's what you do:

1. **Push the pause button (covered in Chapter 6).**

2. **Take time to evaluate the proposed compromise based on all the other basics.**

   If splitting the difference means $125, figure out whether $125 is an acceptable resolution to the negotiation.

3. **If the number is not acceptable, explain why this seemingly fair approach doesn't work.**

4. **If the number is acceptable to you, point out why it is fair based on the facts rather than on the mere fact that it was halfway between the last two positions of you and the other party.**

In the United States, our tremendous sense of fair play dictates that both sides give equally. Following are some rules to live by the next time you're asked to "split the difference":

- Don't fall into the trap of thinking that splitting the difference is the fair thing to do.

- Never offer to split the difference yourself. Instead encourage the other person to offer to split the difference.

- By getting the other party to offer to split the difference, you put him in a position of suggesting the compromise. Then you can reluctantly agree to his proposal, making him feel that he won.

The hidden agenda

One of the most maddening and puzzling experiences is negotiating with someone who has a hidden agenda. The most common hidden agenda I have run into over the years is when the person on the other side of the table has a competition with, an axe to grind with, or favors to curry with someone else in the company. He or she wants to get even, do in, or to win favor with this other person. Of course, you don't know anything about that, so you are negotiating the deal in a straight-ahead fashion, but you can't figure out why this person won't agree to a certain reasonable point, no matter what you do.

To deal with hidden agendas, try the following steps:

1. **Ask a lot of probing questions to find out what is really going on.**

   Doing so requires patience and time. Sometimes, the person on the other side of the tale isn't entirely aware of why he or she is behaving in a certain way.

2. **Try to help the other party with his or her goals without jeopardizing the deal you are after.**

3. **Be sure to follow through with whatever help you can provide.**

   You will make a friend for life at the same time that you close the negotiation on acceptable terms.

Addressing Red Flags That Come Up When It's Time to Close

Up to this point, I've been talking about trying to get the deal closed in spite of a number of annoying tactics that might be thrown at you. What about the situation where the other person has been pleasant to deal with and there have been no real problems — you even have grown to trust the person — but something tells you not to take the person up on his or her last suggestion. The situations in the following sections should make you run for cover.

In some very special situations, signs may indicate that you should go forward with the deal, but those situations are very rare. When you think you are in such a situation, be sure to talk it over with others who will be affected. Never decide to go forward in one of the following situations without getting a reality check from someone you trust and who is knowledge-able in the field.

"If you accept this price, I'll have a lot more work for you in the future"

Well, isn't that enticing. This offer implies more business to come and that the future work will be at a price that is a bit closer to your asking price than this project. Yes, a volume of work usually comes with a discount, so it's reasonable to provide goods or services at a lower price when more units are being purchased. So this is an acceptable arrangement, and you should go forward.

Wrong!

Agree to this deal only if the following points are true:

- ✔ **You get the commitment to future business in writing.** The last thing you want to do is to give a big break on some initial work and never get the payoff of future business that was so artfully dangled under your nose.

- ✔ **You know exactly how much future business there will be and exactly how much of it will come your way.** That's the only way that you will know exactly how big a discount to give off your normal price.

- ✔ **You can afford to do the work or provide the goods at the lower rate.** If you lose money on a job, you can't make it up on volume. You must have a profit in each job you do. So no matter what, you have to go back to the drawing board to be sure that you won't lose money on the initial order.

"We're in such a rush, why don't we start without a contract?"

You have agreed on all the major points, and you trust this guy. Besides that, everyone knows that legal eagles can take forever to get the paperwork out. If you insist on a written contract before you start the project, you're going to come off as an untrusting jerk. So this arrangement will work out, and you should take the plunge.

Wrong!

If the project or services are of any significance, you want, need, and deserve something in writing. Nothing prevents future misunderstandings as much as having things down on paper. The agreement doesn't have to be long and fancy. It doesn't have to be prepared by lawyers. All you need is a simple piece of paper that says, "This is the work I would like you to do" or "These are the goods that I would like you to deliver at such and such a price." You only need a few minutes to prepare such a memo, but you'll need hours or months to untangle misunderstandings that arise when such details aren't clear from the start.

I could write from here to the end of the book about the misunderstandings that arise from failing to make clear at the beginning both parties' expectations. Sometimes unclear communication at the beginning of the negotiation causes the misunderstandings. Sometimes a change of heart during the process creates misunderstandings. Sometimes things don't turn out as expected, which leads to misunderstandings, and no one knows exactly how to handle the new situation.

What causes the misunderstandings really doesn't matter. The important thing is that most of them can be easily and quickly avoided. You simply need to jot down what you think the deal is on a piece of paper and have the other person read it carefully, ask any questions, make any changes, and then sign or initial it. It's a few minutes of your time, but it can save you hours of headaches.

"We're such good friends, let's get started right away"

This is a particularly dangerous situation because no alarm bells go off. You want to go forward. Your friend wants to go forward. What's to stop all of this from happening and happening in the most glorious burst of productivity between friends that the world has ever seen?

When you are dealing with friends — especially old friends — you don't need a written memo. You two have never had a cross word pass between you. You have been through thick and thin. You know what your expectations are, and your friend will always stick by you. In fact, if you mention that you want a memo, it could affect the friendship, and you certainly wouldn't want that to happen.

Wrong again!

Nothing is worse than the misunderstandings that arise between friends who decided to launch a business venture together. The misunderstanding is quickly smothered by feelings of betrayal and loss. It's a mess.

You don't need to make a big deal of putting your agreement in writing. You just say, "Let me just write this all out so I'm clear," and then get the other party to approve it. If the friend you are intending to work with is reluctant to sign such an informal, short form agreement, find out why and thank your lucky stars that you took the time to do this before getting too far into the business venture with him or her. Until you are both on the same page with your expectations and your conceptions of what is and is not acceptable, you shouldn't be making an agreement.

If you two are really friends, don't lay the friendship on the altar of expeditiously making a business deal that is fundamentally flawed. Work out the details up front or move on. It would be much better to keep the friendship outside of a troubled business than to get started on a business venture that is doomed from the beginning because the founders have markedly different ideas about how things are going to work.

Dealing with a Bad Negotiating Environment

A whole cluster of problems that aren't caused by a counterpart can throw a negotiation off track. More often than not, these environmental glitches are as frustrating to the opposing party as they are to you. You can often engage the other side in the solution, unless the problem is bigger than both of you.

Sometimes glitches are not individuals but barriers characteristic of certain businesses. It always takes longer to get a final decision out of a large corporation than it does to get a decision out of a sole proprietorship. It's just the way the world works. However, you can cure some of the glitches that are a product of the corporate culture as opposed to the individual or division that you are negotiating with. In time, you'll know which circumstances you just have to accept and which ones you can change. Following are a few examples of frustrations that you can help to clear away, even though they may be an inherent part of doing business with the company in question.

✔ **Absent key people:** You and your counterpart set a meeting, and another key player has to participate. But just before the meeting is scheduled to take place, something always comes up that keeps that person from attending, so you have to reschedule — again and again and again.

   Solution: See if you can go ahead without that person, and then create a report so the person knows what discussions took place, even though he or she wasn't present at the meeting. Alternatively, see if that person can attend by telephone. Don't let somebody else's calendar prevent you from moving forward on a deal, even if that someone else happens to be your boss.

✔ **Missing information:** Often co-workers put a lower priority than you would like on a piece of work that you need for your negotiation. Sometimes the information just isn't available yet. In the film business, it is hard to negotiate salaries until you get an approved budget. In a manufacturing concern, you may need a production schedule to know when something is to be delivered. Lacking key information can really hold things up.

   Solution: Try to find details you and your counterpart can agree on while waiting for the key piece of information. If your side is holding things up, see how you can help pull the necessary information together. I know, I know. It's not your job. Guess what. Your job is to close the negotiation. If that means helping someone else out so you can get the necessary facts or figures in a timely fashion, so be it. It's frustrating, but better to give a hand than to lose a deal.

✔ **Too much paper:** So many completed forms are necessary that your buyer turns off. Too many demands for duplicate information may irritate the person to the point where he or she gets frustrated and wants to deal with someone else.

   Solution: Fill out as much of the paperwork as possible before you arrive. Have the paperwork well organized. Carry a clipboard so signing is as convenient as possible. Don't solve the problem by having someone sign a blank form.

✔ **Hidden policies:** These directives are hidden from you —
not from the other person. What you don't know can kill
you — or at least kill your deal. If the company's policies
are against you, all the persuasion in the world won't
change things.

Solution: Do your homework. Ask questions. Don't
ignore the situation. You can spot this problem when you
simply aren't making any headway.

✔ **Poorly designed tools and resources:** If you reach for
the contract to close the negotiation and the document
isn't there, the delay may halt the negotiation. Even if
you do have the contract but it's full of typographical
errors or is outdated, the situation spells unprofessional-
ism, and the negotiation is a no-go.

Solution: Check over all the materials you plan to use in
your presentation in advance. Make sure that they are
the best they can be, even if you have to reach into your
own pocket to improve them. Your commission or the
advancement of your career is at stake. If the document
is a form that the company supplies, make the necessary
corrections before you start your negotiating session.

Sometimes frustrations originate in your company, sometimes
in the other person's company. Be sure you try to soften the
impact of these types of problems no matter which company
is the source of the problem. Your job is to close the negotiation, not to play the blame game on corporate environments.

Managing Conflict When the Deal Won't Close

The potential for conflict is an ever-present reality when trying
to close a deal. It can manifest itself in differences of views,
opinions, personality, and interests. But conflict doesn't have
to be destructive. If the right options are chosen to handle conflict the result can be a huge benefit to both sides.

Following are four options that can really help you to manage
conflict when the deal won't close and two options that will
make things worse. Let's start with the two options that tend
to exacerbate the situation and that you want to avoid:

- ✔ **I Win, You Lose.** You just dig in your heels and won't budge. This approach is risky because you come off as a bully to the other party, causing him or her to harbor resentment. This negotiating strategy is based on the belief that you are not responsible for the conflict and therefore will not budge at all to the other side. You must be seen to win. When you use this approach on others, you encourage them to find ways to use "win-lose" back on you.

- ✔ **I Lose, You Win.** You just yield the point without getting anything in return. Do not consider the "I lose, you win" approach to conflict as a strategy. This approach is the route to letting others have their way. Sooner or later they will come back for more, ruining the balance of the negotiation.

Let's turn to some things that might work for you:

- ✔ **Push the pause button.** Here it is again — another instance to use the pause button. Sometimes taking a breather during a heated situation is the best thing to do. It helps cool the situation and keeps you from making unrealistic concessions or demands.

- ✔ **Finding a win-win solution.** This is the best strategy to pursue to manage conflict. When you think with a win-win mentality and act with a win-win attitude, both parties can reach some accord. A win-win solution to conflict encourages constructive conflict, which means you don't have to destroy the other party in order to come out on top.

- ✔ **Mediation.** This approach is recommended only if absolutely necessary. Basically, you continue the negotiation with the help of a third party, such as an attorney. It is often suggested to resolve a negotiation glitch, especially in labor union talks. It never should be considered as an alternative to negotiations in the first place. It's costly and time consuming. Always try to settle matters yourself.

- ✔ **No deal.** A no-deal outcome to a conflict means that nothing changes. There is no advantage for you in continuing the negotiation, so you walk away. Make sure you have alternatives to fall on back when you choose not to make a deal.

The Ultimate Glitch: Someone Walks Away

No glitch presents quite the challenge as when someone walks away from the negotiation. This ultimate glitch has the potential to be final. This sensitive situation also raises questions about how to get things going again. Walking away includes such modern equivalents as slamming the phone down or sending a searing e-mail stating emphatically that the negotiations are over. Obviously, the negotiation is over if the parties don't start talking again. Knowing how to handle these situations can help you keep the deal alive.

If the other party walks away

If you believe that the other party is walking away impetuously or for effect, don't be afraid to make a lunge and pull him or her back. Shopkeepers have held onto marginal sales for centuries by grabbing the arm of a departing customer.

If your counterpart abruptly severs all contact with you by making a hasty exit from the office, slamming down the telephone receiver, or refusing to answer telephone calls, you may be unable to reestablish communications immediately. If the person you're negotiating with gets out of range, use the time to your advantage. Consider the limits you set (see Chapter 2). Go over all the new information gathered since the start of the negotiation. If, upon reflection, you believe that reopening the negotiation makes sense, do so. Don't stand on pride.

The important thing is to keep your eye on your own goals, needs, and limits. If you didn't prepare thoroughly or you skipped setting limits, it's easy for pride or panic to rear its ugly head at this point. Use this unplanned break to evaluate, regroup, and prepare some more.

The breakdown of a negotiation is no time for emotion; it's a time for enlightened self-interest. DeToqueville, the French observer of American life, identified enlightened self-interest as one of the hallmarks of social and business structure in America. Don't let it fail you now. Keep a steely eye on what you want in life. And never be too proud to pick up the phone and get things back on track, if that's what it takes to achieve your personal goals.

If the other party comes crawling back

If the other party calls, be open to finding new ground. If the other person comes back to you, be sure to respect the opening comment, whatever it is. The first comment could even be a negative remark about your own conduct. You can honor the comment with an "I understand," rather than argue over who caused the blow-up. After all, the other party is calling to continue the negotiation, and this is good news.

Even if the other party doesn't come as far as you want, be sure to acknowledge the willingness to make a first step. Under such circumstances, the smallest step may involve a major effort — and may be the key to a final settlement.

When negotiations begin again in earnest, don't dwell on the fact that you went to extremes to enable it to happen. This is not a time for hard feelings or for self-congratulations. Just go forward with the business at hand. Be glad you managed your way through the rough waters.

Be cautious of your limits, which you have determined not to step over, regardless of what's being offered. If you reach the breaking point of your limits, you must be able to walk away and evaluate your other options. If you don't walk away, you lose credibility, and both sides know it. But again, it all boils down to what are you willing to accept, and do you have acceptable alternatives that can carry you through the day? Only you can answer that question.

If one of your competitors walks away

If you and one of your competitors are in negotiations to win the same project and your competitor walks away from the negotiation, move swiftly to close your own deal. Usually, the party on the other side of the negotiation is a bit vulnerable at this time, so you have a good opportunity to obtain a favorable result.

Try to find out all you can about the recent events. Usually the opposing party is your best source. "What the heck happened?" usually brings out more information than you need. Listen. Be sympathetic, even if the person speaking acted a bit unreasonably. Being a strong supporter of your counterpart is one of the best ways to close your own deal.

In the course of listening, try to find out exactly what your counterpart needed that your competitor didn't provide. Find out what both parties had on the table when things blew up. Be sure that the party you are courting is willing to deal with you and won't just use your offer as a club to close the other deal. All of these things are better learned by sympathetic listening as opposed to direct questions. Direct questions can feel too much like cross-examination. (Go to Chapter 3 for tips on asking the right questions.)

Another good source of information is the party that walked away, although this strategy holds several risks. Most importantly, your call may just cause that party to try and get back into the game. At this point, that person is more your competition than the person across the table from you. In addition, the person you are now negotiating with may not like your getting too cozy with the person who just walked away. Be careful about trying this tactic.

Speed is often as important as thorough preparation in this situation. Move quickly to establish communications. Try to listen lots and speak little until you are ready. You already know what you are willing to do in the situation. If you can do so comfortably, make an offer within the range that the other side wants. Close your deal as quickly as possible.

If you're the one walking away

When you negotiate for something, whether the transaction is purchasing a new home or interviewing for a new job, think about the possibility of being unsuccessful in the negotiation. Imagine reaching an impasse and deciding that your best course of action is to terminate the discussion.

This exercise prepares you emotionally for the possibility of not reaching a satisfactory conclusion. It also gives you a sense of walking away from the negotiation and stimulation to think about what would happen next.

Anytime you feel that carrying out an agreement would compromise your integrity or you distrust the other party, run — don't walk — away from the negotiation. Your reputation is the most important thing you have in life. No deal is worth risking your reputation for honesty and integrity.

When you are giving up some long-range goal for a short-term gain, you need to look very carefully at the trade-off. It is seldom worth it, and you should think seriously about walking away unless you can build something into the deal that preserves your ability to pursue your long-range goals.

Starting All Over Again

When you or the other party walks away from the negotiation, your first instinct will probably be to keep walking. Unless you are a runner. Then your instinct will probably be to run.

But hold everything. Don't burn any bridges. Don't destroy a business relationship and a business opportunity over what just may be a temporary hiccup between you and the person on the other side of the table.

Consider the broader context. In the big scheme of things, is it better or worse for your company to have the deal that just fell apart? Consider the other players involved in the negotiation. You've probably worked with them before. Would you like to work with them again?

You may be able to complete what you originally intended if it's something worth doing. Push the pause button (see Chapter 6). Take a break and look at the negotiation as objectively as possible. If that doesn't provide a clear answer to the question of whether to try to put the deal back together, ask a friend or trusted colleague to help you see the different components of the negotiation as you talk through them.

Only you and your inner circle can decide if you should go forward with the deal or if you should let it go. It is a deeply personal decision.

If you decide to go forward, ask yourself a few pertinent questions before rushing back into the fray. Did the previous negotiation fall apart because of a particular sticking point? How would this negotiation differ from the one that broke apart? How did you contribute to the problem?

Before reaching out to the other side to start things up again, check yourself on the six basic skills discussed in this book:

- ✔ Is there anything more you need to know about the other party or the marketplace (or yourself, for that matter)? Find out before you launch another round of talks. Prepare for this negotiation just as diligently as you prepared the first time. Knowing that you are prepared allows you to be present in the moment and be attentive to what is happening during these new negotiating sessions.

- ✔ Are your goals and your limits appropriate? Don't blame the other guy 100 percent. Maybe you were a bit off kilter with your own expectations.

- ✔ Did you listen to the needs and wants of the other side, or did you just plow forward with what you wanted to get out of the deal?

- ✔ Were you clear in your presentation, or could the other side have misunderstood you?

- ✔ Did you use your pause button to take breaks when necessary, or did you get a bit testy with the other party? If you voiced your frustration, don't skimp on the apologies. Keeping your emotions in check is particularly important when you are restarting something that has already gone south once. Save your emotions for another time.

- ✔ Were you trying to close the deal along the way, or did you leave too many items open, so that the other side was a bit overwhelmed? If you jump back into this negotiation, wrap things up bit by bit moving steadily toward a final solution.

When you first try to get things started again, propose one or more solutions. Explain how you want to overcome the previous snag or what you need others to do. Don't spend a lot of time justifying what you need and want — just ask for it. If questioned about your reasons, be prepared to explain them.

At the first session where you start negotiating again, appreciate the other team and yourself. Recognize the fact that you are sitting in the same room with the same party you were negotiating with before. You found a way to ease a difficult situation and get the other party back in the room. Thank those who accommodated your needs. Also take some time to appreciate yourself for creating the circumstances that support your goals and values.

The process of breathing life into a dead negotiation, although difficult, may make you a stronger person. Everyone should learn from their mistakes. In this situation, you may be learning from others' mistakes. Lucky you. The opportunity to conclude a negotiation that has gone seriously off-track doesn't come along that frequently, so take advantage of it.

Chapter 9

Blind Negotiating via Telephone and E-Mail

In This Chapter

▶ Getting through to the right person

▶ Negotiating tips for phone and e-mail

*N*egotiating over the telephone or e-mail is never as good as negotiating in person. Unless you are very careful and very clever, telephone conversations rob you of much of the data that comes to you almost automatically during a face-to-face meeting. The gestures, the facial expressions, the side-long glances between members of the other party — all these are lost in the telephone negotiation.

Negotiating over e-mail is even more difficult. You have no human interaction. Your computer prevents you from hearing a voice or seeing a facial expression. It is also a distraction as you read other e-mails in your inbox or surf your favorite web-sites. Regardless, negotiating via e-mail is fast and saves time, so people do it anyway. If you fall into that category, at least be aware that as good as the Internet is for finding or sending information, it is terrible as a tool of persuasion.

This chapter covers some special considerations you must remember when you use the telephone or e-mail to negotiate. All the other aspects of negotiation are still in play, so don't ignore the rest of the book just because you are using the tele-phone or the Internet. If anything, those other parts become more important.

Putting in the Call

The higher up a person is on the corporate ladder, the more his or her time is protected by others. You may have to get past various staff members who screen calls. Sometimes, all the skills of negotiating the deal are necessary to get a *screener* to let you through or at least put you at the top of someone's call-back list.

Getting past the gatekeeper

Often, you are unable to get through to the right person on the first call. If you want to enjoy maximum success on the phone, you should treat *gatekeepers* — the assistants who take your calls — with the same respect that you treat their bosses. When you are on the phone with an assistant, the assistant is every bit as important as the person he or she works for.

By and large, after the receptionist, the assistant you talk to first has the support and confidence of the person you want to contact. Give the assistant the same respect and confidence you would give the person you're trying to reach. You get through the screening process more often, and you can make progress even when you speak only to the support staff. You don't always have to talk to the boss to get things done.

- ✔ **Don't wear out your welcome.** You find that you get much more accomplished by working as much as possible with assistants and support personnel. Always recognize that until you have established your relationship with the boss and the gatekeeper, the gatekeeper is unable to respond to any of your requests without approval from the boss.

- ✔ **See if the assistant can answer minor questions before you ask the boss.** You don't need to talk to the boss for every single thing that is going on in your negotiation, especially if the negotiation is protracted. If you want to know when to expect a report that was promised yesterday, you can ask the assistant — nicely. If the boss has completed his or her work, the assistant probably knows better than the boss when you can expect the finished product.

- ✔ **Don't get cute, coy, or flirtatious with the gatekeeper.**
  This sleazy approach demeans both parties in the conversation. Respect carries you further in the work-a-day world than all the sexual charm you may think you exude over the phone.

- ✔ **Be businesslike in all your dealings.** Using the name of the assistant, especially to the assistant, is very positive. Always write down the names of key support staff. The calendar system on my computer has several spaces for phone numbers for each person, so I use one of these spaces to fill in the assistant's name.

Leaving a message

Always leave a message, even if it's just your name and phone number. Let the other person know that you cared enough to call. If someone is taking down the message for you, make your comments brief. If you're recording the message on voice mail, you can include more detail, but still be concise. Pack in the information in as few words as possible and be logical.

You are most likely not the only caller on the voice mail. Getting through a string of messages is time-consuming. Getting through a string of long, wordy, and detailed messages is plain annoying. You may have the option of reviewing your message and rerecording it, but you may not. So avoid rambling and leave a message that makes your point in a concise way.

To add importance to your message and avoid playing phone tag, you may want to ask when you can call back. If that doesn't work, give two or three times when you can be reached. One of these approaches is almost certain to work. Arranging a time for the next call elevates your importance and engages the assistant in making the next call the one that connects with the boss. Remember, no one can be more helpful or harmful to you than a seasoned gatekeeper.

With state-of-the-art wireless technology now readily available, most business people can be reached anytime, anywhere. Cell phones and *PDAs* (personal digital assistants that can be used as cell phones, web browsers, personal organizers, and latte makers — okay, that last one's not true . . . yet), make leaving a message, either by voice or by text, a simple task.

Hitting "O"

After you have left your nice succinct message, don't just hang up. Hit "0." This action usually transfers you to a receptionist who can tell you if the person is even in that day or to an assistant who may be able to help you.

The most time-consuming part of a phone call is getting yourself ready to exchange information and then initiating the call. The phone conversation lasts only a few moments, so you need to make every call worthwhile. Make the best use of the time as you can.

Wording your voice mail greeting

You've left a message, and now the person is calling you back. If you aren't in the office, what is the other party going to hear, and is it going to be helpful?

How many times have you heard, "I'm either away from my desk or on the other line"? In today's world, no one wants to wait for much of anything. Even if you don't have an imaginative message, at least eliminate the obvious. I'm always impressed with the tailored message. Most of the people who work on the *For Dummies* series change their messages frequently. "Today is _____, and I will be in meetings most of the day, so I probably won't get back to you until tomorrow. Please leave a message." That type of message gives you information you can use.

Assembling the Participants for a Telephone Chat

Deciding who participates in a telephone negotiation is as important as choosing whom to invite to an in-person meeting. Conference calling no longer reduces you to one-on-one negotiations over the phone. Not everyone has had face-to-face conversations with each other. Voices will not always be easily identifiable, so the fewer people, the better.

After you decide on the participants, choose the best way to gather these people together. The following sections describe the three basic choices.

Gathering in front of the telephonic campfire

If one or two other people within your organization need to be included in the conference, invite them into your office and use the speakerphone. That way, at least the two or three of you who are together don't lose the benefit of sharing gestures, documents, and facial expressions.

Depending on the size and style of your office, conferencing capabilities vary. Larger companies with high-tech offices often have the most recent, state-of-the-art conferencing equipment. For smaller offices, a good conference phone is essential and may not need to be as elaborate.

Using conference calling saves you the time of having one conversation and then calling someone else to repeat the same message. Conferencing also maximizes accuracy of communications and prevents delays. Because all parties are hearing the same thing, everyone's confidence level in the negotiation is at its highest.

Hiring outside help

When you don't want to deal with the hassle of connecting several parties through your own private phone system, arrange a formal conference call through the telephone company. You can do this through a private provider or, in many large companies, through a dedicated conference line. These approaches are especially useful if the participants are to be on the line the entire time rather than for just a small portion of the conversation. You can be confident that the call will be well coordinated and all participants will be clearly heard.

Making the Most of Your Telephone Negotiation

The biggest disadvantage of telephone negotiation is that the convenience of the telephone can cause people to devalue the importance of the negotiating session. In a face-to-face meeting, the parties gather all the materials they could possibly need during the conversation, drive across town, battle the parking problem, find their way to a particular office or conference room, take time to pour a cup of coffee, find a seat, and begin the conversation. After this effort, everyone knows the meeting is important.

Frequently, when negotiators save time by using the telephone, instead of putting some of that time back into the actual discussion, they hurry through the conversation as if it were less important than if they had spent unproductive time commuting and getting settled in. You can restore importance to the conversation by making a formal appointment to talk rather than calling the person out of the blue. What you have to say is important. Don't let the importance of what you have to say be scuttled on the shoals of time. Take the necessary time to let the other party know that you have something to contribute.

Never lose sight of the fact that every communication is important during a negotiation, whether by telephone, letter, or face-to-face discussion. Take care of the conversational niceties and then some, even if you don't have to drive across town to have the meeting.

Crisp beginnings

Before you go into an important meeting, you take a beat to be sure that you look your best. You automatically check your hair, your collar, or your teeth (especially if you had spinach for lunch). Do the same on the phone. If all you do is take a deep breath and put a smile on your face, you feel more prepared, and the telephone session begins much better.

Always put your best foot forward, even if no one can see your feet. When you start a telephone negotiation, give the same attention to a good first impression that you give to a face-to-face meeting. How you answer the phone or initiate the call is important. Too many people just pick up the phone and say "Yeah?" or some other perfunctory greeting. Don't be rude. Start with a positive greeting, "Good morning," "Good afternoon," or "Thanks for calling." It sets a positive tone. If you don't have time to talk, ask the caller if you can arrange another convenient time. If you are the caller, ask if the time is convenient. Arranging another time shows respect. And you must give it to get it.

When the meeting starts

If time or circumstances force you to conduct important negotiations over the telephone, try your best to compensate for the lack of face-to-face interaction with careful listening and pointed questions. Keep in mind the disadvantage of the phones as not having the visual cues that are inherent in a face-to-face conversation.

You can turn the telephone into a negotiating instrument almost as effective as the face-to-face meeting by tuning into the tone and tempo of the other person's speech. This aware-ness gives you a powerful advantage in a day in which the telephone is probably used more frequently than face-to-face meetings in business negotiations.

The person on the other end of the line can't see you either, so give lots of auditory feedback. In a face-to-face meeting, looking out the window and contemplating your next thought is perfectly acceptable. However, on the telephone the people on the other end of the line can't see what you're doing. They're likely to think that you've been disconnected or that you are distracted. They may ask, "Are you still there?" If someone asks you that, you know that she was concerned enough to stop what she was saying to check on you. That interrupts her train of thought. Maintain your presences with verbal cues, but don't fall back on "Uh-huh, uh-huh." Simply acknowledge periodically that you are listening and under-standing what the other person is saying.

Speaking with authority

Because you only get one chance to make a first impression, develop your *vocal personality*. The first impression you make over the phone depends entirely on how you speak. Begin to listen to yourself by working with a voice recorder. Pay attention to these characteristics:

- ✔ **Volume:** Others must be able to hear you clearly. You don't want the listener straining to hear your soft voice or holding the phone away because you are irritatingly loud.

- ✔ **Pronunciation:** Others must be able to understand you. The word "five" cannot sound like the word "fine." Speak clearly. Speak slowly. Never mumble — especially not over the telephone. Mumbling can be corrected by putting energy and lip motion into your voice. If you're not excited or enthusiastic about what you're saying, fake it.

- ✔ **Rate:** Speak at a moderate pace — not too fast or too slow.

- ✔ **Intonation:** Avoid a monotone. Let your voice rise on important words and lower on the not-so-important ones. You don't need to be sing-songy, but a variety of inflection adds interest to your speech.

- ✔ **Nonwords:** Look out for the "ums" and "uhs." These fill silence, but a short pause is so much better. Don't be afraid of the silence.

- ✔ **Emotion or tone:** This element is hard to define, but you know it when you hear it. It's the emotion or attitude in your voice — the edge you put on certain words. When you say, "I've told you before," your tone can convey that you are angry, condescending, or defensive. Saying the words differently ("*I've* told you before") can convey that you are friendly, happy, or nonjudgmental. Put a smile on your face to put a smile in your voice.

Questions to ask on the telephone

Some good questions are designed to close the sensory gap imposed by the phone. The questions are easy; you've probably heard them before. If you thought they were polite inquiries, you were only partly correct. Add these questions to your telephone routine:

- ✔ **"How are you doing today?" and "Is this a good time to talk?"**

 These two classic inquiries serve one purpose: Taking the temperature of the person with whom you are speaking. Don't rush right into a negotiation — find out whether the person you want to negotiate with is ready.

✔ **"Do you have a half hour or should we schedule a phone appointment?"**

This inquiry is a more-sophisticated version of the first two questions. If you know the phone session is going to be long, check with the other person's schedule first. Don't draw someone unwittingly into a long session. Also, scheduling a phone appointment elevates the importance of the conversation and allows for better preparation.

✔ **"Do you have the file on your desk?" and "Do you need to get anything else before we go ahead?"**

If you refer to a document, find out whether the other party has the document in hand. Be sure that you are both working with the same version of the document. If a question exists, try to fax or e-mail the version under discussion during the conversation. Faxing or e-mailing any missing documents while you are on the phone is essential for clarity. It also gives you a certain authority and power. Making sure everyone has the necessary paperwork tells the other party that you are in charge because you want to make sure this session is as productive as possible.

✔ **"I hear a change of tone. Is everything okay?" and "You sound down today."**

These are two classic ways to articulate what you suspect is true. Go ahead and put words to what you hear. Do the same if you hear that someone has become distracted or started munching a late lunch. Noting such a distraction permits the person on the other end of the line to ask you to repeat whatever was missed — and surely something was missed. It acts as a bridge back into the negotiation. These comments also dissuade such conduct. People aren't likely to turn away from the conversation if they know that you are aware each time they do so.

As your listening skills improve, you may find that you can hear some of the facial expressions you don't see. If you are that good at listening, let the other person know. Your insight is flattering to them and helps confirm the information you are receiving.

Shaking hands over the phone

At the end of a negotiating session, you wrap it up. If the deal has not closed, you walk the person to the door and arrange the next session. Finally, you look the person in the eye, say good-bye, and shake hands.

 You cannot shake hands on the phone, but you can use words as though you are shaking hands. Recall the walk to the door at the end of your last face-to-face session. You almost always have a mini-conversation about something other than the business you were discussing. Try to do the same thing on the phone.

Too often, the efficiency of the phone works against using closing pleasantries. Fight that instinct. Take the extra moment. Try to end on a personal, positive, or forward-looking note. The specific communication is a function of your personality and your relationship with the other person. Whatever closure you use face to face at the end of a negotiating session, you should try to use at the end of a telephone negotiation.

Negotiating via E-Mail

The Internet and e-mail have revolutionized communication. For better or worse, the Internet is a fast and easy way to gather and transmit information, so it is very good for communicating facts. Sending e-mail across the Internet is not nearly as useful for persuading people to do something or to agree to something or to get out of your way so you can do something. Therefore, e-mail is best used to transmit documents and other information. Use a more personal approach to change minds.

Negotiating through e-mail is iffy for many of the same reasons. You can't hear the tone of the person you are negotiating with, and you can't read body language or facial expressions. Add to that the ease of forwarding information that you'd rather keep under wraps, and you could have a real problem on your hands.

Of course, e-mail has a role in modern negotiating. E-mails are an incredibly efficient way to be sure everyone with a need to know receives all the information in a timely fashion. But be wary of trying to persuade someone using e-mail. It works sometimes, but it's always better to pick up the phone when it's time to change someone's mind about something.

The next sections offer tips for how to make the best of an e-mail negotiation.

Plan

Before you begin an e-mail communication, think about the purpose of the e-mail. What's your agenda? Reading through dozens (or hundreds) of e-mails is time consuming, so strive to be as brief as possible. Summarize your objectives and be direct. Don't bore your reader with long-winded messages.

Keep these questions in mind when planning an e-mail communication:

✔ What information do you want to share?

✔ Who needs to know? Be sure you have the proper name(s) and e-mail address(es) for the person(s) you e-mail.

✔ Are you sending the e-mail *internally* (to someone within the office) or *externally* (to someone outside the office)? Internal e-mails, usually between colleagues, tend to be less formal. Niceties are not necessarily required. External e-mails usually require more thought and careful planning.

Organize

An e-mail's organization is equivalent to your appearance before a meeting. First impressions make all the difference. Consider the points in the following list when you're organizing an e-mail message:

✔ **Start with a meaningful subject line.** The *subject line* summarizes the point of your message. It's the first thing the reader sees. A good subject line allows your reader to properly sort and prioritize his or her e-mails. Make sure your subject line is short and informative.

- ✔ **Use bullet points to highlight main points.** This makes your e-mail message easy to scan and gets your message across.

- ✔ **Be concise and to the point by keeping sentences and paragraphs short.**

- ✔ **Consider the look of your e-mail.** Avoid fancy, colorful backdrops for your e-mails. Instead, use a white background. Make the message easy on the eyes. Keep in mind that negotiating via e-mail does not require any artistic talent.

- ✔ **Watch the color and size of your fonts, again making sure both are consistent and straightforward.** Nothing is more distracting than having some words appear larger or smaller than others or color coordinating your paragraphs.

- ✔ **Be sure not to overuse CAPITALS.** Remember, tone is difficult to gauge in an e-mail, and using capital letters shifts the weight of words and meanings into something unintended. Additionally, if you write a message using all uppercase letters, it seems as if you are shouting. This may trigger an unwanted response from your reader.

- ✔ **Avoid abbreviations and e-mail lingo.** Common e-mail abbreviations, such as "btw" (by the way), "lol" (laugh out loud), "ttyl" (talk to you later), "fyi" (for your information) and so on, are okay between friends or during a quick chat. In a negotiation, they are usually viewed as unprofessional and can be distracting. And, btw, they take away from the formality of your e-mail . . . as do emoticons. :)

- ✔ **Always reread your message before sending, and always check for spelling and grammatical errors.** A well-written e-mail signifies preparedness.

Exercise "reply" principles

Replying to an e-mail is equally as important as initially composing and sending one out. Be as thorough and direct as you are with messages that you initially compose. Some things to consider when replying to an e-mail message:

✔ **Are you responding with emotion or with fact?** Pay close attention to your e-mailed response before sending. If the initial e-mail was written with formality, respond with similar care and thoughtfulness.

✔ **Have you answered all questions asked?** Stick to the topic of the message and answer questions that you are asked. Sometimes, when a lot of information is sought or many questions are asked, it is better to go into the body of the e-mail and answer them in the order that they are posed by the sender. You can distinguish your answers with colors or italics.

✔ **Is the message thread still intact?** A *message thread* is the way each e-mail is added to all the preceding e-mails so that anyone receiving the very latest e-mail can check over the entire communication history, if need be. Leaving the message thread intact saves the recipient time and frustration in searching for related e-mails. If the thread is maintained, you can delete the prior e-mail each time a new one comes in.

✔ **Is this e-mail urgent?** Try to avoid writing "Urgent" in your subject line unless your message truly is urgent. The high-priority tab on most e-mail systems is enough to note the urgency of a message.

Pick up the phone

When all else fails and an e-mail negotiation stalls, pick up the phone. Communicating via e-mail can sometimes serve as an impasse in a negotiation. For one, you are not physically present in a room with another party, so you are prone to procrastinate and not respond to e-mail. Also, if frustration sets in during a stalled e-mail negotiation, you can't gauge the level of frustration.

You also want to pick up the phone at the beginning of a negotiation. It's really hard to establish rapport with someone solely through e-mail contact. Even with a significant time difference that will favor greater e-mail use, start with the phone to introduce yourself to the other person.

Chapter 10

Ten Personality Traits of Top Negotiators

In This Chapter
▶ Recognizing the qualities of a great negotiator
▶ Developing those qualities yourself

*I*n my negotiating seminars, participants often ask what personality traits they need to develop to attain more positive outcomes. So here is a list.

Nobody has all the traits listed in this chapter. As you look over the list, find those that apply to you and develop them further. Find those qualities that you feel are completely absent from your personality and work on them to improve your negotiating style and your life. You can use all the personal qualities here, developing them as fully as you like, at your own pace, and in your own way.

Empathy

Empathy is the ability to participate in another's feelings or ideas, to put yourself in another's shoes. Empathy is listed as the first trait for a reason: It's the bedrock of all successful communication and a necessary trait for great negotiators.

You can improve your empathetic response by writing out a list of behaviors, values, and goals that you can't possibly agree with, but you *can* acknowledge that *others* feel that way. Next to each behavior, write "but I understand that *they* feel that way."

Some of the traits listed in this chapter are virtually impossible to develop without first honing your sense of empathy. Being empathetic also helps you maintain your own identity as you experience the views and emotions of others, because it enables you to recognize the differences between you and the person you are talking to.

Respect

Respect follows closely on the heels of empathy. First, you must have respect for yourself and the limits you set. Only then will you be able to respect or consider worthy other people and the limits they set.

Respect for yourself is another, more specific way of saying self-confidence.

Respect is reciprocal in negotiations: If you give it, you are much more likely to get it.

Personal Integrity

By *personal integrity,* I mean honesty and trustworthiness — qualities necessary for others to trust you and place their confidence in you in a negotiation.

How can you begin to develop integrity right now?

- ✔ Follow the rules of society — even the smallest ones.

- ✔ Keep agreements with yourself and others. If you promise to send along a pile of information, send it along. And do it without delay and without waiting for a reminder.

- ✔ Never misrepresent anything in a negotiation. Not replying to a certain question or divulging certain information is completely acceptable; lying is not.

Honest and trustworthy people take ownership for their lives, choices, thoughts, feelings, and actions, without blaming or faulting others. They know their deepest values and don't depend on their position for power.

Fairness

Fairness is another trait based on empathy. You must believe that the needs and wants of other people are worth considering, along with your own.

To develop fairness, consider what your goals are and what the goals are of the other party. Delineate areas of agreement and areas that need compromise. Always keep in mind the ability and experience of the person with whom you are dealing.

Patience

Patience means bearing pains or trials calmly without complaint. It's the ability to tolerate frustration and adversity on the way to reaching your goals — and not give up. Everyone grew up hearing, "If at first you don't succeed, try, try again." It's absolutely true — collecting the "no's" is part of getting a "yes." All successful people know that getting knocked down, refused, denied, and blocked is part of life. Success comes to those who are steadfast and keep going.

Responsibility

Being *responsible* means exhibiting reliability or dependability. Being responsible means that you accept the consequences when tasks are completed or neglected.

Being responsible doesn't mean that you won't make mistakes; it does mean that you will correct them when you realize you've made them. One way to improve in this area is to take care of the little (or big) problems for which you are responsible, so you have a clear space to get on with achieving goals.

Flexibility

Flexibility is the ability to deal skillfully and promptly with new situations and difficulties. If one approach doesn't work, you can try another. Life's problems and the problems of a negotiation are seen as challenges to overcome.

Flexibility is at the heart of closing a deal in a way that satisfies each side and is workable in the real world. You must be flexible in a negotiation to fit your goals and needs with the goals and needs of the other party.

Sense of Humor

Having a sense of humor involves looking for the comic quality in a seemingly serious situation — the ability to perceive, appreciate, or express what is amusing or comical. Finding humor in adversity helps you get on with finding solutions rather than blaming others. A prerequisite is self-respect and the flexibility to take a creative view of an imperfect situation.

Self-Discipline

Self-discipline is at the heart of the ability to lead a self-reliant, self-sufficient life. If you are self-disciplined, you don't need someone "on top of you" to motivate you. You have internal forces that drive you toward your goals, and your rewards come from within you, rather than from people externally reinforcing you.

Stamina

Stamina is the ability to keep going when others have dropped by the wayside. To increase your stamina, do the following:

- Eat right.
- Take your vitamins.
- Sleep enough and well.
- Try to find balance in your life between work and play.
- Meditate.

Needless to say, stamina is a hallmark of all great negotiators. You can't win the game if you don't have the stamina to stay in the game.

Index

• N •

negative comments, avoiding, 76
negative tactics. *See also* obstacles
　in negotiations
　bluffing, 61–62
　changing positions, 108–109
　double messages, 112–113
　good cop, bad cop ploy, 109–110
　hidden agenda, 115–116
　"I'm going to be honest with you"
　　tactic, 76
　invisible partner, 110–112
　"more work in the future" tactic,
　　116–117
　nickel and diming, 113–114
　slurs, 76
　"split the difference" tactic,
　　114–115
　starting without a contract,
　　117–119
　"take it or leave it" tactic, 76
　"trust me" tactic, 75–76
negotiation. *See also specific topics*
　alternative options for, 21–22, 90
　closing a deal. *See* closing a deal
　complexity of, 14
　described, 1, 5
　by e-mail. *See* e-mail negotiations
　gender differences in, 14–17
　international, 17–18
　learning from, 34–35, 87–88,
　　104–105, 127–128
　pausing. *See* pausing a
　　negotiation
　practicing, 9, 24–25, 71
　skills required for. *See* skills
　starting over, 104, 124, 126–128
　by telephone. *See* telephone
　　negotiations
　walking away from. *See* walking
　　away from a deal
nervous laugh, interpreting, 50–51
nickel and diming, 113–114

Nierenberg, Gerard I. (author)
　*How to Read a Person Like a
　　Book,* 62
nonverbal communication. *See*
　body language
notes, taking. *See also* written
　communication
　to create a pause, 79–80
　to improve listening process,
　　45–46
　of nonverbal signals, 53
　when others are interrupting, 69

• O •

objections, addressing, 102–104
obstacles in negotiations. *See also*
　walking away from a deal
　changing of positions, 108–109
　conflicts, managing, 121–122
　documents, flaws in, 121
　double messages, 112–113
　fears causing, 72, 88–89, 101–102
　good cop, bad cop ploy, 109–110
　hidden agenda, 115–116
　hidden policies, 121
　"I'm going to be honest with you"
　　tactic, 76
　information missing, 120
　invisible partner, 110–112
　key people are absent, 120
　materials, flawed, 121
　"more work in the future" tactic,
　　116–117
　nickel and diming, 113–114
　objections to deal, 102–104
　paperwork, excessive, 120
　preparing for, 107–108
　reasons for, 12
　resources, inadequate, 121
　slurs, 76
　"split the difference" tactic,
　　114–115

• *P* •

• W •

walking away from a deal
ability to, importance of, 28
celebrating after, 106
communicating to other party
when, 25–27
competitor walking away,
124–125
incentives for, 21
other party walking away,
123–124
reasons to, 125–126
starting over after, 126–128
WAR (worry, anger, resentment),
88–89
Warning! icon, 4
win-win negotiating, 92, 94, 122
women
differences in negotiation style,
14–15
negotiation skills for, 15–16
work environment problems,
119–121
worry, anger, resentment (WAR),
88–89
written communication
abbreviations in, 67, 140
alternative options, listing, 22
for changing of positions, 109
clarity in, 67–68

contract. *See* contract
distractions, listing to remind
yourself later, 45
e-mail negotiations, 139–140
flaws in, 121
goals, listing, 9
journalistic techniques for, 68
letter to other party after walking
away, 26–27
limits, listing, 23, 28
memo to other party confirming
negotiations, 46
notes. *See* notes, taking
presentation materials. *See*
presentation materials
term definitions in, 30
written contract, 97. *See also*
contract

• Y •

"yeah, but" response, 44
yourself
fears, overcoming, 72, 88–89,
101–102
goals, knowing, 7, 66
hot buttons, identifying, 11, 83–84
reputation, maintaining,
26, 106, 126

Math & Science

Algebra I
For Dummies,
2nd Edition
978-0-470-55964-2

Biology
For Dummies,
2nd Edition
978-0-470-59875-7

Chemistry
For Dummies,
2nd Edition
978-1-1180-0730-3

Geometry
For Dummies,
2nd Edition
978-0-470-08946-0

Pre-Algebra Essentials
For Dummies
978-0-470-61838-7

Microsoft Office

Excel 2010
For Dummies
978-0-470-48953-6

Office 2010 All-in-One
For Dummies
978-0-470-49748-7

Office 2011 for Mac
For Dummies
978-0-470-87869-9

Word 2010
For Dummies
978-0-470-48772-3

Music

Guitar
For Dummies,
2nd Edition
978-0-7645-9904-0

Clarinet For Dummies
978-0-470-58477-4

iPod & iTunes
For Dummies,
9th Edition
978-1-118-13060-5

Pets

Cats For Dummies,
2nd Edition
978-0-7645-5275-5

Dogs All-in One
For Dummies
978-0470-52978-2

Saltwater Aquariums
For Dummies
978-0-470-06805-2

Religion & Inspiration

The Bible
For Dummies
978-0-7645-5296-0

Catholicism
For Dummies,
2nd Edition
978-1-118-07778-8

Spirituality
For Dummies,
2nd Edition
978-0-470-19142-2

Self-Help & Relationships

Happiness
For Dummies
978-0-470-28171-0

Overcoming Anxiety
For Dummies,
2nd Edition
978-0-470-57441-6

Seniors

Crosswords
For Seniors
For Dummies
978-0-470-49157-7

iPad 2 For Seniors
For Dummies,
3rd Edition
978-1-118-17678-8

Laptops & Tablets
For Seniors
For Dummies,
2nd Edition
978-1-118-09596-6

Smartphones & Tablets

BlackBerry
For Dummies,
5th Edition
978-1-118-10035-6

Droid X2 For Dummies
978-1-118-14864-8

HTC ThunderBolt
For Dummies
978-1-118-07601-9

MOTOROLA XOOM
For Dummies
978-1-118-08835-7

Sports

Basketball
For Dummies,
3rd Edition
978-1-118-07374-2

Football
For Dummies,
2nd Edition
978-1-118-01261-1

Golf For Dummies,
4th Edition
978-0-470-88279-5

Test Prep

ACT For Dummies,
5th Edition
978-1-118-01259-8

ASVAB For Dummies,
3rd Edition
978-0-470-63760-9

The GRE Test
For Dummies,
7th Edition
978-0-470-00919-2

Police Officer Exam
For Dummies
978-0-470-88724-0

Series 7 Exam
For Dummies
978-0-470-09932-2

Web Development

HTML, CSS, & XHTML
For Dummies,
7th Edition
978-0-470-91659-9

Drupal For Dummies,
2nd Edition
978-1-118-08348-2

Windows 7

Windows 7
For Dummies
978-0-470-49743-2

Windows 7
For Dummies,
Book + DVD Bundle
978-0-470-52398-8

Windows 7 All-in-One
For Dummies
978-0-470-48763-1

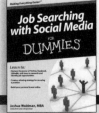

Available wherever books are sold. For more information or to order direct: U.S. customers visit
www.dummies.com or call 1-877-762-2974. U.K. customers visit www.wileyeurope.com or
call (0) 1243 843291. Canadian customers visit www.wiley.ca or call 1-800-567-4797.
Connect with us online at www.facebook.com/fordummies or @fordummies